PREACHING HELPS:
OUTLINES, ILLUSTRATIONS, AND POEMS

PREACHING HELPS: OUTLINES, ILLUSTRATIONS, AND POEMS

by
CARL G. JOHNSON

BAKER BOOK HOUSE
Grand Rapids, Michigan

PHOTOLITHOPRINTED BY CUSHING - MALLOY, INC.
ANN ARBOR, MICHIGAN, UNITED STATES OF AMERICA
1978

FOREWORD

In the midst of a busy evangelistic schedule, the author of this book of outlines, illustrations, and poems has prepared this material, with the sincere prayer that it may be useful to other speakers as they "Preach the Word. . . . " and " . . . persuade men. . . . " It's a real joy to know that " . . . it pleased God by the foolishness of preaching to save them that believe."

The author presents in this book many of the outlines which he uses in his evangelistic and conference ministry, plus illustrations and poems which he has selected from *literally* thousands of them which he has read. (The outline is on the left side of the double page, while the *appropriate* illustration and poem is on the right side of the double page.) He wishes to thank the authors and publishers for the illustrations and poems that are used and he has tried to give credit to the proper persons. May God bless them for their contribution.

The outlines are only suggestive and there should be much study and prayer by those who use them before they are used. Let everyone feel free to use anything in this book for the glory of God.

The author desires to express his hearty thanks to Carole Bowling for her devoted service in typing the manuscript, and to John Bowling for his help in preparing the manuscript for publication.

Most of all, he wants to thank God for His assistance and guidance, and his prayer is " . . . that He might be glorified."

CONTENTS

UNIT I
A GOOD MAN'S HARD TO FIND
Acts 11:24

The Bible makes it plain that all men by nature are sinners (Rom. 3:23); that "...there is none that doeth *good*, no, not one" (Rom. 3:12).

The Bible also makes it plain that when God saves a man by grace through faith in Jesus Christ (Eph. 2:8, 9), that man can become a *good man*. In Acts 11:24, God says of Barnabas, "For he was a *good man*, and full of the Holy Ghost and faith...." I want to give you seven marks of a *good man* found in the Bible.

I. A GOOD MAN HAS A GOOD BEGINNING.

In order for a man who is not good by nature to become good, he must be born again. When a man believes on the Lord Jesus Christ and receives Him as personal Saviour and Lord, God gives him the power (or right) to become a child of God (John 1:12, 13).

II. A GOOD MAN PROFESSES A GOOD PROFESSION — I Timothy 6:12.

Every man who receives Christ as Saviour and Lord should confess Him openly (Rom. 10:9, 10; Matt. 10:32, 33).

III. A GOOD MAN DOES GOOD WORKS — Ephesians 2:10.

A good man is "created in Christ Jesus unto good works..." (Eph. 2:10).

IV. A GOOD MAN HAS A GOOD CONSCIENCE — I Peter 3:16.

God wants us to "have always a conscience void of offense toward God, and toward men" (Acts 24:16).

V. A GOOD MAN LIVES A GOOD LIFE — I Peter 3:16.

The word "conversation" in this verse means "manner of life."

VI. A GOOD MAN FIGHTS A GOOD FIGHT — I Timothy 6:12.

The Christian has three main enemies — the world, the flesh, and the devil. He must put on the whole armor of God and take his stand and fight a good fight against these enemies (Eph. 6:10-18).

VII. A GOOD MAN IS A GOOD STEWARD — I Peter 4:10.

We have been entrusted with the Gospel (I Thess. 2:4); with talents (Matt. 25:14-29); with money (II Cor. 9:6, 7); and with our bodies and lives (Rom. 12:1; I Cor. 6:19, 20).

A GOOD MAN IN THE PHILIPPINES

B. H. Pearson shares this story:

It was a great day in a small mountain church in the Philippines, when twenty-three adults and young people confessed their faith in Christ by baptism.

At the conclusion of the service, a visitor, Angel Taglucop, congratulated the minister. "You must be exceedingly happy to have so many new believers enter the fellowship of your church today."

"Of course I am, but I'm not the person most responsible for this group being ready for membership today. Seventeen of these twenty-three have come because one man visited their homes and prepared them for membership through prayer and Bible study. He's sitting back there on the last bench."

Mr. Taglucop went back to talk with this remarkable steward of the Gospel, and immediately noticed that one of the man's legs was several times normal size. Amazed that the man could have visited seventeen people whose homes were all in the steep mountain regions, he asked, "How can you manage with that leg?"

"God gives me strength to drag it along," was the simple reply. "But I hid in these mountains during the war," protested Mr. Taglucop. "I know how steep the trails are." The man replied: "Then you know how God provides us with roots and saplings to pull ourselves along."

Mr. Taglucop then advised the man to go to a hospital and have his leg treated before it was too late. When he heard that this treatment would take several months, the man shook his head. "There is no time. You see, there are seven more families in the mountains to whom I must first bring the gospel."

This earnest witness died soon thereafter, on his way up a mountain to visit one of those homes. Is it any wonder that such a man had this tremendous influence in the lives of these seventeen converted men? How long since we risked anything to win a soul for Christ? Do we really care?

FULL-HEARTED MEN!

Give me full-hearted men, who love their Lord, with a sparkle and
    flash in their eye,
  Who are ready to fight, to work, to win, who are ready to do, or to
    die.
Men full of grace and the Holy Ghost are the men we must have
    today;
  Full-hearted, strong-hearted, cross-bearing men, who will valiantly
    lead the way!   — Paul Martin

UNIT II
THE BEST ADVICE A MOTHER EVER GAVE
John 2:5

Napoleon said, "Let France have good mothers, and she will have good sons." Spurgeon said, "I cannot tell how much I owe to the solemn words and prayers of my good mother."

Good mothers are always giving good advice to their children. I thank God for the good advice my mother has given me in my lifetime.

Mary, the mother of Jesus, gave the best advice any mother ever gave. She said, concerning her Son, Jesus Christ, "Whatsoever he saith unto you, do it" (John 2:5). No better advice could be given than this — to do whatsoever Jesus says unto us. Here are some of the things He says to us; may God help us to " . . . do it."

I. JESUS SAYS, "REPENT" — "DO IT."

In Mark 1:15 Jèsus commands, "Repent ye. . . . " and in Luke 13:3 He says, "except ye repent, ye shall all likewise perish." (See also Acts 17:30; 20:21; II Peter 3:9.)

II. JESUS SAYS "BELIEVE THE GOSPEL" – "DO IT."

In the same verse that Jesus said, "Repent ye . . . " He follows it by saying "and believe the gospel" (Mark 1:15). (See also I Cor. 15:1-4; Rom. 1:16; John 3:14-18, 36; Acts 16:31.)

III. JESUS SAYS, "CONFESS ME BEFORE MEN" — "DO IT."

Jesus makes it clear in Matthew 10:32, 33 the importance of confessing Him before men. (See also Rom. 10:9, 10).

IV. JESUS SAYS, "PRAY" — "DO IT."

He instructed His disciples to pray for laborers to be sent into His harvest (Matt. 9:38). (See also I Thess. 5:17.)

V. JESUS SAYS, "GIVE" — "DO IT."

He reminded His followers: "freely ye have received, freely give" (Matt. 10:8). (See also Luke 6:38.)

VI. JESUS SAYS, "GO" – "DO IT."

He commanded, "Go ye into all the world, and preach the gospel to every creature" (Mark 16:15). (See also Matt. 28:19, 20; Acts 1:8.)

VII. JESUS SAYS, "LOVE ME, KEEP MY COMMANDMENTS" — "DO IT."

He made it plain that if we really loved Him, we would keep His commandments (John 14:15, 21, 23). Take this mother's advice — "Whatsoever he saith unto you, do it." Jesus said, "If ye know these things, happy are ye if ye do them" (John 13:17).

A MOTHER WHO FOUND HER NICHE IN LIFE

Many years ago there lived in the city of Dublin a beautiful and talented young lady, the wife of a young captain. The young captain was fatally wounded in a duel, and the young lady became a widow before she was eighteen. First she tried solitude to rid herself of her grief, then she tried the gaieties of life — but all in vain. One morning, early, she went down to the river to take her life.

Just as she was about to take the fatal plunge, she saw in a distant field a farmer ploughing. He called to his horses and whistled cheerily as he followed the plough; and she said bitterly, "Happy man! He has something to live for; he has a niche to fill." And there came to her a message as from God: "You have a niche to fill, too. You have life, talents, opportunities. Why throw them away?" Turning from the river bank, she hurried home, saved from a suicide's death and doom. Soon afterwards, upon hearing a sermon on John 3:16, she received Jesus Christ as her own personal Saviour. Some time later, she married a fine Christian man and into that home was born a son. The mother, realizing her niche was to train that child for God, brought him up in the nurture and admonition of the Lord. That son was Dr. Grattan Guinness, who was mightily used of God in leading thousands to Christ in the British Isles in the great revival of 1859. Grattan Guinness later got the burden of world evangelization and began training young men for Christian service on the mission fields of the world.

The mother of Grattan Guinness, in bringing up her son for God, probably did more for God's kingdom than all the great statesmen of her century.

Every mother who trains her children for God is doing a service, the value of which only eternity will reveal.

A MOTHER'S PRAYER

I wash the dirt from little feet, and as I wash I pray,
    "Lord, keep them ever pure and true to walk the narrow way."
I wash the dirt from little hands, and earnestly I ask,
    "Lord, may they ever yielded be, to do the humblest task."
I wash the dirt from little knees, and pray, "Lord, may they be
    The place where victories are won, and orders sought from Thee."
But soap and water cannot reach where Thou alone canst see.
    Her hands and feet, these I can wash — I trust her heart to Thee!

UNIT III
THE BIGGEST LIAR IN THE WORLD
John 8:44

I have met many big liars in my lifetime, but the biggest liar I have ever met is the devil, of whom Jesus spoke in our text, "he is a liar, and the father of it." Let me point out some of the lies of "The Biggest Liar in the World."

He says:

I. "THERE IS NO DEVIL."

The devil wants you and me to think there is no devil. Many people today believe his lie and make fun of anyone who does believe in him. Billy Sunday said, "I know there is a devil for two reasons: First, the Bible declares it; and second, I have done business with him." Yes, there is a devil. Don't believe his lie. (See Gen. 3:1-15; Matt. 4:1-11; 25:41; Eph. 4:27; 6:11; II Tim. 2:26; Heb. 2:14; James 4:7; I Peter 5:8; Rev. 12:9, 10-17; 20:2, 7-10.)

II. "THE BIBLE IS NOT GOD'S WORD."

The devil said to Eve, "Yea, hath God said . . . ?" (Gen. 3:1). Don't believe his lie — the Bible *is* God's Word. (See Mark 13:31; John 12:48; I Tim. 3:16; II Peter 1:21.)

III. "YOU'RE NOT SO BAD."

He wants you to think that you are a good person. Don't believe his lie — God says we are all bad. (See Isa. 53:6; Jer. 17:9; Rom. 3:9-19.)

IV. "GOD IS TOO GOOD TO SEND ANYONE TO HELL."

He has multitudes of people believing this lie. Don't you believe it — there is a Hell and many are going there. (See Ps. 9:17; Matt. 5:22, 29, 30; 10:28; 11:23; 16:18; 18:9; 23:15, 33; Mark 9:43, 45, 47; Luke 10:15; 12:5; 16:19-31; Rev. 20:10-15; 21:8.)

V. "YOU WON'T BE ABLE TO HOLD OUT AS A CHRISTIAN."

Thank God, when we put our trust in Jesus Christ, He holds us. (See John 6:37, 10:27-29; Rom. 8:35-39; Phil. 1:6; Jude 24.)

VI. "THERE IS TOO MUCH TO GIVE UP TO BECOME A CHRISTIAN."

This is one of his biggest lies. Think of what we *get* when we are saved. (See Rom. 6:23; 8:32; Eph. 1:3; Tim. 6:17.)

VII. "YOU HAVE PLENTY OF TIME TO GET SAVED."

This is perhaps his biggest lie — don't believe it. You may not have another minute. Trust Christ and be saved *now*. (See Prov. 27:1; II Cor. 6:2.)

THE DEVIL AND HIS HELPERS

Oswald J. Smith relates this interesting story:

A man dreamt that he saw Satan seated on his throne, and all his evil spirits gathered round him, waiting for his commands.

Suddenly the question was asked by their master: "Who will go forth to ruin souls on earth?" The answer came readily enough from one: "I will."

"What will you tell them?" Satan responded. "I'll tell them that there is no God," was the answer.

"That will not do," he said gloomily. "Men know there is a God."

Again he asked the question: "Who will go forth to ruin souls?"

"I will," a second spirit replied. "And what will you tell them?" Satan asked. "I'll tell them that there is a God; that He is a just and a holy God, and that they are too bad to come to Him," he replied.

"That won't do," repeated Satan. "Their very need will drive them to Him. Besides, while there are Bibles left in the world, they have only to read how God invites them."

Once more the dreamer heard the terrible question ring through the courts of darkness: "Who will go forth to ruin souls?"

There was a pause. At last a third spirit repeated the words: "I will."

"And what will you tell them?"

"I'll tell them," he answered slowly, "that there is a God. I will let them hear the gospel as often as they like. I'll tell them that it is all true, but, I'll tell them there is time enough, to think about accepting God's offer."

There was a murmur of applause, and then, "Go forth," said the Prince of Darkness; "you will be successful." He went forth, and is daily deceiving thousands.

FAIR QUESTIONS ABOUT THE DEVIL

Men don't believe in a devil now, as their fathers used to do;
   They forced the door of the broadest creed, to let his majesty
      through.
Who spoils the peace of the world today with the fiery breath of Hell?
   If the devil isn't, and never was, won't somebody rise and tell:
Who dog the steps of the toiling saint and digs the pit for his feet?
   Who sows the tares in the field of time wherever God sows His
      wheat?
The devil was fairly voted out, and of course the devil is gone,
   But simple people would like to know: who carries his business on?

— Victoria Selin

UNIT IV
THE CHURCH WHICH PEOPLE WERE AFRAID TO JOIN

In Acts 5:1-10 we read of the judgment of God upon a man and his wife for lying to the Holy Spirit. Within three hours' time from the death of Ananias, his wife, Sapphira, was stricken dead and because of this judgment, "... great fear came upon all the church, and upon as many as heard these things" (Acts 5:11). Then we are told, "And of the rest durst [dared] no man join himself to them ..." (Acts 5:13). Here was a church which people were afraid to join, if they were not right with God. The characteristics of this church are given in Acts 4:31-33.

I. IT WAS A PRAYING CHURCH — "And when they had prayed ..." (v. 31a).

II. IT WAS A SPIRIT-FILLED CHURCH — "and they were all filled with the Holy Ghost ..." (v. 31b).

III. IT WAS A WITNESSING CHURCH — "and they spake the Word of God with boldness" (v. 31c).

IV. IT WAS A UNITED CHURCH — "And the multitude of them that believed were of one heart and of one soul ..." (v. 32a).

V. IT WAS A SHARING CHURCH — "they had all things common" (v. 32b).

VI. IT WAS A POWERFUL CHURCH — "And with great power gave the apostles witness of the resurrection of the Lord Jesus ..." (v. 33a).

VII. IT WAS A FAVORED CHURCH — "And great grace (favor) was upon them all" (v. 33b).

This is the kind of church God uses to win souls. Through this church and its people "believers were the more added to the Lord [not joined to the church], multitudes both of men and women" (Acts 5:14).

A church is made up of people, so these seven characteristics of a church should be what characterizes our lives. May God help us to be praying, Spirit-filled, witnessing, united, sharing, powerful, and having God's grace upon us.

Charles G. Finney said, "Christians are more to blame for not being revived than sinners are for not being converted."

PRAYER FOR POWER FOR THE PREACHER

A. M. Hills tells the story of a church which prayed for their preacher and how he became a powerful preacher and how the church became a powerful church:

Wilbur Chapman often told of his experience when he went to Philadelphia to become pastor of Wannamaker's church. After his first sermon an old gentleman met him in front of the pulpit and said, "You are pretty young to be pastor of this great church. We have always had older pastors. I am afraid you won't succeed. But you preach the gospel, and I am going to help you all I can."

"I looked at him," said Dr. Chapman, "and said, here's a crank.'"

But the old gentleman continued: "I am going to pray for you that you may have the Holy Spirit's power upon you, and two others have covenanted to join with me."

Then Dr. Chapman related the outcome. "I did not feel so bad when I learned that he was going to pray for me. The three became ten, the ten became 20, and the 20 became 50, and 50 became 200, who met before every service to pray that the Holy Spirit might come upon me. In another room the 18 elders knelt so close around me to pray for me that I could put out my hands and touch them on all sides. I always went into my pulpit feeling that I would have the anointing in answer to the prayers of the 219 men.

"It was easy to preach, a very joy. Anybody could preach with such conditions. And what was the result? We received 1100 into our church by conversion in three years, 600 of them men. I do not see how the average pastor, under average circumstances, preaches at all.

"Church members have much more to do than go to church as curious idle spectators, to be amused and entertained. It is their business to pray mightily that the Holy Ghost will clothe the preacher with power and make his words like dynamite."

THE PERFECT CHURCH

I think that I shall never see a Church that's all it ought to be:

A Church whose members never stray beyond the Strait and Narrow Way;

A Church that has no empty pews, whose Pastor never has the blues,

A Church whose Deacons always deak, and none is proud, and all are meek;

Such perfect Churches there may be, but none of them are known to me.

But still, we'll work, and pray and plan to make our own the best we can.

— Selected

UNIT V
THE DEDICATED LIFE
Romans 12:1, 2

M. R. De Haan, in speaking of dedication, said, "Thousands of believers have been saved and have ALL of the Holy Spirit, but have never allowed the Holy Spirit to have ALL of them.... What is needed is a once-for-all dedication of our lives, a full surrender to Christ, a final enthroning of Christ in the heart, as Lord and Master. ... Dedicate your life to Him once and for all, never to be repeated."

In these two verses in Romans 12 we have:

I. THE APPEAL TO DEDICATION.

A. By God — "I beseech you, therefore, brethren...." God begs those who are Christians to give Him their bodies.

B. By God's Mercies — "By the mercies of God...." Because of all of God's mercies — justification, sanctification, identification, preservation, glorification — God urges us to present our bodies to Him for His use.

II. THE ACT OF DEDICATION.

A. Is to be voluntary — "present," or put at one's disposal.

B. Is to be personal — "ye" ... "your."

C. Is to be sacrificial — "living sacrifice."

D. Is to be holy — "holy," which means "set apart for God," "devoted to the use of."

E. Is acceptable to God — "acceptable unto God," or well-pleasing to Him.

F. Is to be definite — "make a decisive dedication" (Williams translation; A.N.T.).

G. Is to be complete (body — Rom. 12:1; members — Rom. 6:13; self — II Cor. 8:5).

H. Is to be final — "once for all offer" (Williams translation); "once for all presentation" (Wuest).

III. THE ACHIEVEMENT OF DEDICATION.

A. There will be separation — "And be not conformed to this world..." (Rom. 12:2a).

B. There will be transformation — "be ye transformed..." (Rom. 12:2b).

C. There will be illumination — "that ye may prove what is that good, and acceptable, and perfect, will of God" (Rom. 12:2c).

"I DON'T HAVE VERY MUCH TIME LEFT"

Some years ago at a church conference, I closed a series of messages by speaking on this theme: Your body is the temple of God; He desires to dwell in it, possess it, and use it for His purposes in the world. When I had finished, because it was the closing of the weekend conference, I invited any to stand who wished to present their bodies as living sacrifices unto the Lord. The first person to rise quickly to her feet was a very lovely, elderly woman. Another older woman, then an older man, after which many others rose. I was curious because I had been impressed with this lady who was lovely and unusually gracious; so as soon as possible I made my way to her and asked, "Do you mind telling me why you so quickly stood to your feet this evening when I gave that invitation?"

Her answer was this, "Dick, I am eighty-eight years old, and I have been a church member all my life, but I never knew until tonight that God wanted my body, and I stood quickly because I don't have very much time left!"

— Richard C. Halverson

TRUE DEDICATION

Thou hast no tongue, O Christ, as once of old,
  To tell the story of Thy love divine;
The story's still the same, so sweet, so true,
  But there is no tongue to tell it out — but mine.

Thou hast no hands, O Christ, as once of old,
  To feed the multitude with bread divine;
Thou hast the living bread, enough for all,
  But there is no hand to give it out — but mine.

Thou hast no feet, O Christ, as once of old,
  To go where Thy lost sheep in sorrow pine;
Thy love is still the same, so deep, so true,
  But now Thou hast no feet to go — but mine.

And shall I use these ransomed powers of mine
  For things that only minister to me?
Lord, take my tongue, my hands, my feet, my heart,
  And let me live, and love, and give for Thee.

UNIT VI
DON'T BE IGNORANT

At least seven times in the New Testament, God says, "I would not have you ignorant," or something to that effect — (Rom. 1:13; 11:25; I Cor. 10:1; 12:1; II Cor. 1:8; I Thess. 4:13; II Peter 3:8). God is saying to us, "Don't Be Ignorant."

I. DON'T BE IGNORANT ABOUT SALVATION.

God said of the Jewish people, "For they being ignorant of God's righteousness, and going about to establish their own righteousness, have not submitted themselves unto the righteousness of God" (Rom. 10:3). Not only are Jewish people ignorant of God's righteousness, or salvation, but I find many people everywhere I go who know nothing about how to be saved. About 85 to 90 per cent of American people who are not saved, do not know how to be saved, according to polls that have been taken.

God's Word teaches that "There is none righteous, no, not one" (Rom. 3:10), and " ... all our righteousnesses are as filthy rags ... " (Isa. 64:6). In order for us to be saved, God requires a perfect righteousness, which we do not have. But thanks be to God, that which God requires, He provides through His Son, Jesus Christ. When we receive Jesus Christ as our personal Saviour and Lord, we are " ... made the righteousness of God in him" (II Cor. 5:21). "Believe on the Lord Jesus Christ, and thou shalt be saved ... " (Acts 16:31).

II. DON'T BE IGNORANT ABOUT THE SAINTS.

In I Thessalonians 4:13-18, God tells us that Christians who have died will rise from the dead when Jesus descends from Heaven, and Christians who are still living when Christ returns will be caught up together with the saints who have died and " ... so shall we ever be with the Lord." God does not want us to be ignorant of this wonderful truth.

III. DON'T BE IGNORANT ABOUT THE SECOND COMING.

II Peter 3:8-15 tells us that God doesn't count time as we do, " ... that one day is with the Lord as a thousand years, and a thousand years as a day," and the reason Christ has not returned yet is because of the longsuffering and patience of God. Christ may return at any moment and we should be prepared for His coming. "Therefore be ye also ready: for in such an hour as ye think not the Son of Man cometh" (Matt. 24:44).

I WAS A HEATHEN IN AMERICA

Dorothy C. Haskin tells of her ignorance of God's way of salvation:

Though I grew up in the United States, I was as much a heathen as any savage in darkest Africa. My mother's parents had been Protestant, and after a marriage which ended in divorce she was attracted by the promises of the cults which flourished in so-called Christian America.

Mother went from Christian Science to Unity, to Theosophy, to Numerology, to Astrology, with a dash of Palmistry, Re-incarnation, and finally Spiritualism.

After vainly searching, believing their false claims without results, when forty-seven, mother in desperation killed herself. She had found nothing in life to satisfy her. The shock of her death sent me searching.

Finally, weary, I telephoned a nearby church and, unwilling to hear the minister preach, I asked if they had a week-day Bible class. They had. I attended it, and was surprised to learn that just because one is born does not make one a child of God. It makes us creatures, but, "As many as received him, to them gave he power to become the sons of God, even to them that believe on his name" (John 1:12).

My next question was, "Believe what?" That, "All have sinned and come short of the glory of God" (Rom. 3:23).

It was not hard to search my heart, and find sin there, but what should I do with it? I found the answer in Romans 10:9 — "That if thou shalt confess with thy mouth the Lord Jesus, and shalt believe in thine heart that God hath raised him from the dead, thou shalt be saved."

Yes, in Christ I was saved, not only from sin, but in Him I found the answer to all my fears and questions. I thank Christ for freeing me from the mumbo-jumbo of heathen cults. "If the Son therefore shall make you free, ye shall be free indeed" (John 8:36).

TRUE WISDOM

True wisdom is in leaning on Jesus Christ, our Lord;
   True wisdom is in trusting His own life-giving Word;
True wisdom is in living near Jesus every day;
   True wisdom is in walking where He shall lead the way.

UNIT VII
ETERNAL THINGS

Over the triple doorways of the Cathedral of Milan are some carvings. Over one is a beautiful wreath of roses, and underneath are these words: "All that pleases is but for a moment." Over another is a cross, and underneath: "All that troubles is but for a moment." But over the great central archway leading into the main aisle is the inscription: "That only is important which is eternal." Here are some "Eternal Things" in the Bible, and they are very important.

I. THE ETERNAL GOD — "The *eternal God* is thy refuge, and underneath are the everlasting arms ..." (Deut. 33:27). (See also Hab. 1:12 and Ps. 90:2.)

II. THE ETERNAL SON — "*In the beginning* was the Word, and the Word was with God, and the Word was God. The same was *in the beginning* with God (John 1:1, 2). The "Word" here speaks of Jesus Christ (John 1:14), who was in the beginning with His eternal Father. (See also Mic. 5:2.)

III. THE ETERNAL SPIRIT — "How much more shall the blood of Christ, who through *the eternal Spirit* offered himself without spot to God ..." (Heb. 9:14).

IV. THE ETERNAL PURPOSE — "According to the *eternal purpose* which he purposed in Christ Jesus our Lord" (Eph. 3:11).

V. THE ETERNAL JUDGMENT, DAMNATION, PUNISHMENT, DESTRUCTION — "*eternal judgment ...*" (Heb. 6:2; Matt. 25:46; Mark 3:29; II Thess. 1:9).

VI. THE ETERNAL FIRE — "suffering the vengeance of *eternal fire*" (Jude 7). (See also Matt. 18:8; 25:41.)

VII. THE ETERNAL LIFE — "the righteous into *life eternal*" (Matt. 25:46); "the gift of God is *eternal life* through Jesus Christ our Lord" (Rom. 6:23).

The "Eternal God," in His "Eternal Purpose," gives "Eternal Life" to those who are brought by the "Eternal Spirit" to put their trust in the "Eternal Son," and they shall escape the "Eternal Judgment, Damnation, Punishment, Destruction and Fire," and shall have an "eternal inheritance" (Heb. 9:15) and "eternal glory" (I Peter 5:10).

"FIRE! ETERNAL FIRE!"

Evangelist Sam Jones related this story in one of his sermons:

In the city of Atlanta, the Wilson House Hotel caught fire some years ago. The servants ran from room to room to awaken the guests. A servant went to one room where there were two men, awakened them. One jumped out of bed, aroused the other, but with a moan and a groan the other man went to sleep again. The guest who was up dressed hurriedly and ran to the bed to shake the other man and said, "Get up, the house is on fire." The other man simply moaned and groaned and went back to sleep. His friend then pulled him out of bed, stood him on his feet and said, "The house is on fire! Hurry, hurry, or you will be burned up!" The man when turned loose fell back into bed with a moan and a groan, and went to sleep again. The next day, as they were raking among the debris of the building, they found his bones all charred and burned. And many a time on earth, Heaven seems to long to arouse us and pull us away from our surroundings and stand us on our feet and cry, "Fire! Eternal Fire!" and yet there we stand, and at last among sulphurous flames and eternal perdition, our bones lie burned and charred forever.

THE MARCH OF TIME

Time marches on, its hurrying feet are sounding down life's busy
    street;
  We listen to their measured beat, time marches on!
Time marches on, its clarion call is heard in hut and palace-hall;
  Though kingdoms rise and kingdoms fall, time marches on!
Time marches on, nor can it stay to wipe the orphan's tears away;
  Nor grief of anguished hearts allay, time marches on!
Time marches on, its steady flight is heralding approaching night;
  And though its locks with age are white, time marches on!
Time marches on — 'twill end some day, when heaven and earth shall
    pass away;
  And then forever and for aye — ETERNITY!
ETERNITY! and time no more shall march along earth's storm-swept
    shore;
  Its toll of years forever o'er — ETERNITY.
ETERNITY! where wilt thou spend that dateless age that has no end?
  O haste and make thy choice, my friend, time marches on!

                    — M. E. Rae

UNIT VIII
THE FATHER WHO IS WORSE THAN AN INFIDEL
I Timothy 5:8

In this verse, God says that a father who does not provide for his own has denied the faith "... and is worse than an infidel." I pray that you will be a father who provides for his own.

A Father should provide:

I. A CHRISTIAN FATHER FOR HIS OWN.

Every father should be a Christian and give his children a Christian father. He has a great responsibility as the head of the house and should resolve as Joshua did: "as for me ... [I] will serve the Lord" (Josh. 24:15). If you are not a Christian father, now is the time to repent and receive Christ (Acts 20:21) and become one.

II. A CHRISTIAN HOME FOR HIS OWN.

His home should be a place where it can be truthfully said: "Christ is the Head of this home ... the Unseen Guest at every meal ... the Silent Listener to every conversation." He should co-operate with his wife to provide a home that is wholesome and happy.

III. A CHRISTIAN EXAMPLE FOR HIS OWN.

He should be a model of what he wants his family to be, and should be a man of whom God could say, as he did of Abraham, "For I know him, that he will command his children and his household *after him,* and they shall keep the way of the Lord, to do justice and judgment ... " (Gen. 18:19).

IV. CHRISTIAN TRAINING FOR HIS OWN.

He should "bring them up in the nurture and admonition of the Lord" (Eph. 6:4), and "Train up a child in the way he should go ... " (Prov. 22:6). God says, "the father to the children shall make known thy truth" (Isa. 38:19).

V. CHRISTIAN ACTIVITIES FOR HIS OWN.

He should make sure that his family activities are Christian in every way, socially, morally, musically, and recreationally.

VI. CHRISTIAN LOVE FOR HIS OWN.

He should love his wife and his children "with a pure heart fervently" (I Peter 1:22).

VII. A CHRISTIAN FAMILY FOR HIS OWN.

He should say, by the grace of God, "as for *me and my house,* we will serve the Lord" (Josh. 24:15), and he should seek to win every member of his household to the Lord.

TWO FATHERS — ONE WHO PROVIDED, ONE WHO DIDN'T

Whenever I speak to parents, two fathers come before me. One lived on the Mississippi River. He was a man of great wealth. One day his eldest boy had been borne home unconscious. They did everything that man could do to restore him, but in vain. Time passed, and after a terrible suspense he recovered consciousness.

"My son," the father whispered, "the doctor tells me you are dying."

"Oh!" said the boy, "you never prayed for me, father; won't you pray for my lost soul now?"

The father wept. It was true he had never prayed. He was a stranger to God. And in a little while that soul, unprayed for, passed into its dark eternity.

The father has since said that he would give all his wealth if he could call back his boy only to offer one short prayer for him.

What a contrast is the other father! He, too, had a lovely son, and one day he came home to find him at the gates of death. His wife was weeping, and she said:

"Our boy is dying; he has had a change for the worse. I wish you would go in and see him."

The father went into the room and placed his hand upon the brow of his dying boy.

"Do you know my son, that you are dying?" asked the father.

"Am I? Is this death? Do you really think I am dying?"

"Yes, my son, your end on earth is near."

"And will I be with Jesus to-night, father?"

"Yes, you will soon be with the Saviour."

"Father, don't weep, for when I get there I will go straight to Jesus and tell Him that you have been trying all my life to lead me to Him."

THE KIND OF DAD I'D BUY

If I went shopping for a dad, here is what I'd buy:
>One who would always stop to answer a little boy's "Why?"
One who would always speak kindly to a little girl or boy,
>One who would give to others a bit of sunshine and joy.
I'd pick a dad that followed the Bible's Golden Rule,
>And one who went regularly to Church and Sunday School.
I'd buy the very finest dad to place on our family tree,
>And then I'd try to live like him so he would be proud of me.

>— Helen Kitchell Evans

UNIT IX
THE FIRST SPACE MAN
Genesis 5:24; Hebrews 11:5; Jude 14, 15

At 9:07 a.m., Moscow time, on April 12, 1961, a twenty-seven-year-old Soviet Cosmonaut, Major Yuri A. Gagarin, soared off a launching pad in a five-ton craft, Vostok I, and has become known as the first space man. Khrushchev said to Gagarin, "You have made yourself immortal because you are the first man to penetrate into space." He orbited the earth only once, in one hour and forty-eight minutes flight time, before landing safely. But in the Bible we read of a man who lived perhaps five thousand years ago who took a trip through space and went much higher than the 203.2 miles Gargarin reached. In fact, he went all the way to Heaven to be with God, for according to Genesis 5:24 and Hebrews 11:5, "God took him . . ." and he "was translated that he should not see death; and was not found, because God had translated him. . . ." This man, Enoch, is really "The First Space Man," and he is mentioned in only three places in the Bible.

I. ENOCH WALKED WITH GOD — Genesis 5:24.
Someone has written a brief biography of him: "He was — for God made him; he was not — for God took him; he is — for God has him."
Alexander Whyte said of Enoch, "He walked abroad every morning with his child in his arms, and with God in his heart. . . . Fathers and mothers, young fathers and young mothers . . . seize your opportunity. Let not another day pass. Begin today. Begin tonight. . . . Take him for example. Follow him in his blessed footsteps in his family life. . . ."

II. ENOCH WAS WELL-PLEASING TO GOD — Hebrews 11:5.
To please God there must be faith in Him and in His Son Jesus Christ (Heb. 11:6).

III. ENOCH WITNESSED FOR GOD — Jude 14, 15.
He spoke of the second coming of Christ and judgment when He comes.

ENOCH WENT HOME TO LIVE WITH GOD

A little girl returning from Sunday School gave, in simple language, her version of Enoch walking with God. She said: "One day God went down to Enoch's house and got acquainted with him.

"Enoch was so happy that God came to see him, that he said, 'I want to walk with you every day.' Then God said: 'All right, come along!'

"So one day Enoch went out to walk with God. They took each other by the hand and walked all day long. They enjoyed themselves so much that Enoch forgot to look at his watch. The sun went down on them.

"Enoch said: 'I will have to spend the night in the woods!' God said: 'Enoch, you are almost at my house. Come, and go home with me.' And Enoch said: 'All right.' And he went. He liked it so good that he never came back."

WALKING WITH GOD

To walk with my Lord is my greatest delight,
    Whether by day or mid darkness of night.
Tho' sin oft allures me, I've chosen aright,
    For I walk by His faith, and not by my sight.
My walk oft times is like Enoch's — alone,
    At times like Jacob's, whose pillow was a stone.
Even like my Master Whose spirit did groan
    When He saw the sin and doubt of His own.
I've chosen the path that my Master has trod,
    I receive the comfort of His staff and rod.
Tho' weary at times and reduced to a plod,
    My greatest delight is to walk with my God.

                    — Rev. B. C. Jennings

UNIT X
FIRST THINGS FIRST
Matthew 6:33

John Wannamaker was one of the great merchantmen of this last century. He was a prominent Philadelphia businessman, Postmaster General of the United States, and Superintendent of the world's largest Sunday School, when someone asked him, "How do you get time to run a great Sunday School, with the business of your stores, your postmaster generalship, and all the other tremendous obligations of your life?" Mr. Wannamaker replied, "Why, the Sunday School is my business. All those other things are just things. Fifty-five years ago, I decided that God's promise was sure: 'Seek ye first the kingdom of God, and his righteousness; and all these things shall be added unto you.'"

In many cases we are "majoring in minor things, and minoring in major things." Consider some things which God puts first.

I. SEEK GOD'S KINGDOM AND RIGHTEOUSNESS — Matthew 6:33.
We owe it to God to put Him first; we owe it to others to put God first; we owe it to ourselves to put God first.

II. BE RECONCILED TO YOUR BROTHER — Matthew 5:23, 24.
To try to worship God, to bring gifts to Him, or to do service for Him, are all in vain if we are not right with our brother.

III. CAST OUT THE BEAM IN YOUR EYE — Matthew 7:1-5.
This means that we are to make sure that our own lives are right before we can help others.

IV. PRAY AND GIVE THANKS FOR ALL MEN — I Timothy 2:1-3.
God's Word tells us that we are to pray for all men and "Pray without ceasing" (I Thess. 5:17).

V. HONOR THE LORD WITH OUR SUBSTANCE — Proverbs 3:9.
God wants the firstfruits, not the left-overs. Are you giving God what's right, or what's left?

VI. JUDGE YOURSELF — I Peter 4:17.
We are to judge ourselves and confess our sins, so that God will not have to chasten us (I John 1:9; I Cor. 11:31, 32).

VII. GIVE YOURSELF TO THE LORD — II Corinthians 8:5.
God's Word speaks about giving ourselves to the Lord (Rom. 12:1).

"SEEK YE FIRST THE KINGDOM OF GOD"

D. L. Moody used this story:

I remember, a number of years ago, I was working out in the field. A man told me something I did not understand. He said that when he left home to make his fortune it was a beautiful morning when he left his mother's door, and she gave him this text of Scripture: "Seek ye first the kingdom of God, and his righteousness; and all these things shall be added unto you" (Matt. 6:33).

He said he paid no attention to it. He walked from town to town, and the first Sunday he was away he went into a little country church, and the minister got up and preached from the text, "Seek ye first the kingdom of God." But he said to himself that he was not going to seek the kingdom of God yet. He went to church in another town, and he hadn't been going there a great while before he heard a sermon from the text, "Seek ye first the kingdom of God, and his righteousness." The sermon and the text made a deep impression on his mind; but he calmly and deliberately said: "I will not seek the kingdom of God now, I will wait until I get rich." He went to another town and went to church there. What was His surprise when the minister got up in the pulpit and preached from the text, "Seek ye first the kingdom of God, and his righteousness; and all these things shall be added unto you." The Spirit strove mightily with Him; but he just fought it — made up his mind that he would not become a Christian until he had become settled in life; and he said that all the sermons he heard since made no more of an impression upon him than upon that stone and he struck it with a hoe. It seemed to him as if the Spirit of God had left him.

I left home, went to Boston, and there I was converted. When I came back home I wanted to talk with him and tell him about the Saviour, but I found out that he had gone to the insane asylum and to everyone who went to see him he would point his finger and say, "Young man, seek first the kingdom of God and his righteousness." Reason had reeled and tottered from its throne, but the text was still there. God had sent that arrow down into his soul.

FIRST THINGS FIRST

No time, no time for study, to meditate and pray —
    And yet much time for "doing" in a fleshly, worldly way.
No time for things Eternal but much for things of earth,
    The things important set aside for things of little worth.
Some things, 'tis true, are needful but first things must come first;
    And what displeases God's own Word of God it shall be cursed.

— M. E. H.

UNIT XI
FIVE THINGS GOD CANNOT DO

You may be surprised to hear that there are some things God canno do, but as you read the Bible, you find that this is so. Young said "God's inability is moral. In the material world He can do everything in the moral and spiritual world God is confronted with glorious im possibilities." Here are "Five Things God Cannot Do."

I. GOD CANNOT LIE.

"In hope of eternal life, which God, that *cannot lie*, promised before the world began" (Titus 1:2). "God is not a man, that he should lie ..." (Num. 23:19). "And also the Strength of Israel will not lie ... (I Sam. 15:29); "it was impossible for God to lie ..." (Heb. 6:18) Thank God, we have a God of truth, who says what He means and means what He says.

II. GOD CANNOT LOOK UPON SIN.

"Thou art of purer eyes than to behold evil, and *canst not look on iniquity* ..." (Hab. 1:13). Of course, God sees sin, but the meaning here is that He cannot approve it, cannot condone it, cannot tolerat it. God always judges and punishes sin — "every transgression and dis obedience received a just recompense of reward" (Heb. 2:2). But He also forgives sin, because Jesus paid the full penalty of sin when He died on the cross, and those who put their trust in Him have God' sure promise: "your sins are forgiven you for his name's sake" (I John 2:12).

III. GOD CANNOT DENY HIMSELF.

"... he *cannot deny himself*" (II Tim. 2:13), which means tha God is faithful and cannot be inconsistent with Himself. He remain true and faithful to His Word and His righteous character.

IV. GOD CANNOT BE TEMPTED WITH EVIL.

"God *cannot be tempted with evil* ..." (James 1:13). God is in capable of being tempted by evil — there is nothing in God that re sponds to sin. "... God is light, and in him is no darkness at all" (John 1:5).

V. GOD CANNOT ENDURE HYPOCRISY.

In Isaiah 1:11-15, God speaks of the empty religious observance of the people, and in verses 14 and 15 He says, "the new moon and sabbaths, the calling of assembles I cannot endure.... your new moon and your hypocritical feasts my soul hates ..." (A.O.T.). Jesus said "God is a Spirit: and they that worship him must worship him in spirit and in truth" (John 4:24).

34

"I'M A GOOD SINNER"

Evangelist Eddie Martin speaks of a woman who responded to an invitation:

A well-dressed woman came forward at the salvation invitation in Bluefield, West Virginia. I took her hand and prepared to give her a prayer to repeat after me. The prayer usually is, "Dear Lord, I know that I am a no-good sinner. I know I can't save myself. I do need forgiveness for my awful sins. I can't do without you, Jesus. Please forgive me for my many sins. I, here and now, receive You into my heart as my personal Saviour. I'll try to live for You from this night on. I pray my prayer in Jesus' name. Amen!"

I took this woman's hand and began to give her the prayer to repeat after me. "Dear Lord, I know I'm a no-good sinner." She never said a word. I looked at her and said, "Don't you want to be saved?" She said, "Yes, I do want to be saved, but I'm not a sinner." "Then you can't be saved," I said. "Jesus died only for sinners." "But, Mr. Martin," she replied, "I'm a good sinner."

"A good sinner! Lady, there are no good sinners. You will have to take your seat. God can't save you until you become conscious that you are a no-good sinner and need His forgiveness." "But, Mr. Martin, you don't understand. I'm really not a bad sinner." Losing my patience with her, I told her to go back and sit down. She held on to my hand with a vice-like grip. Finally she looked me in the eyes and said, "Oh, please forgive me. I know I am a no-good, hell-deserving sinner. I am a proud, no-good sinner. I do need Christ to forgive me of my sins."

"Wonderful! Now, lady, you are ready to do business with God."

GOD CANNOT LIE!

God cannot lie! We can rest assured. His Word is true, through ages
  endured.
  As we are told in His precious Word, iniquity in His sight com-
    pletely absurd.
Evil, in us all, God cannot endure. He's perfect and sinless, and always
  pure.
  Never tempted with evil — evil He loathes, always ready to admit
    those who heed His woes.
"In spirit and in truth" we must worship Him. Deceitfulness in wor-
  ship can only be sin.
  Our God is so mighty, so how can we deny that God is God! Our
    God cannot lie!

— Carole Bowling

UNIT XII
FIVE WONDERFUL THINGS FROM A WONDERFUL VERSE
John 5:24

This is a very wonderful verse which was spoken by Jesus Christ. Harry A. Ironside said of this verse: "Observe . . . there are five links, all of which go together: 'Heareth' — 'Believeth' — 'Hath' — 'Shall Not' — 'Is Passed.'" I would like to show you five wonderful things from it.

I. A WONDERFUL PRIVILEGE — "heareth my Word. . . . "
What a wonderful privilege we have in America, to hear the Word of God. Over half of the world's population have not had this privilege.

"So then faith cometh by hearing, and hearing by the Word of God" (Rom. 10:17).

II. A WONDERFUL PERSON — "Him that sent me. . . . "
This wonderful Person is God the Father, who has sent Jesus Christ His Son into the world that we might be saved.

"For God sent not his Son into the world to condemn the world, but that the world through him might be saved" (John 3:17).

III. A WONDERFUL POSSESSION — "hath everlasting life. . . . "
This is the greatest possession anyone can have and everyone who has really trusted Christ as personal Saviour and Lord has it now.

"He that believeth on the Son hath everlasting life . . . " (John 3:36).

IV. A WONDERFUL PROMISE — "shall not come into condemnation. . . . "
This promise can never be broken. "There is therefore now no condemnation to them that are in Christ Jesus . . . " (Rom. 8:1).

V. A WONDERFUL PASSAGE — "is passed from death unto life."
Until a person is born again, he is dead in trespasses and sins, but the moment he receives Christ, that moment he passes from the state of spiritual death to everlasting life.

"And you hath he quickened [made alive, A.N.T.], who were dead in trespasses and sins" (Eph. 2:1).

GOD SAID IT...I BELIEVE IT...THAT SETTLES IT!

J. Wilbur Chapman tells how he received assurance from John 5:24:

I will tell you how to be saved, and how you may know you are a Christian. I was studying for the ministry, and I heard that D. L. Moody was to preach in Chicago, and I went down to hear him. I finally got into his after-meeting, and I shall never forget the thrill that went through me, when he came and sat down beside me as an inquirer. He asked me if I was a Christian. I said, "Mr. Moody, I am not sure whether I am a Christian or not."

He very kindly took his Bible and opened it at John 5:24, which reads as follows: "Verily, verily, I say unto you, He that heareth my word, and believeth on him that sent me, hath everlasting life, and shall not come into condemnation; but is passed from death unto life."

I read it through, and he said: "Do you believe it?" I said, "Yes." "Do you accept it?" I said, "Yes." "Well, are you a Christian?" "Mr. Moody, I sometimes think I am, and sometimes I am afraid I am not."

He very kindly said, "Read it again." So I read it again.

Then he said, "Do you believe it?" I said, "Yes." "Do you receive Him?" I said "Yes." "Well," he said, "are you a Christian?"

I just started to say over again that sometimes I was afraid I was not, when the only time in all the years I knew him, and loved him, he was sharp with me. He turned on me with his eyes flashing and said, "See here, whom are you doubting?"

Then I saw it for the first time, that when I was afraid I was not a Christian I was doubting God's Word. I read it again with my eyes overflowing with tears.

Since that day I have had many sorrows and many joys, but never have I doubted for a moment that I was a Christian, because God said it.

VERILY, VERILY

Oh, what a Saviour, that He died for me!
　　From condemnation He hath made me free;
"He that believeth on the Son," saith He,
　　"Hath everlasting life."
"Verily, verily I say unto you,"
　　"Verily, verily," message ever new;
"He that believeth on the Son," 'tis true,
　　"Hath everlasting life."

　　　　　　　　　　— G. M. J.

UNIT XIII
"GOD IS SAYING SOMETHING TO US TODAY"
Jeremiah 22:29

George K. Schweitzer, nuclear scientist, said some time ago, "I believe God is saying something to us today. I believe He is either giving us a warning, is preparing a judgment on this country or is preparing a judgment on the world."

Yes, "God Is Saying Something to Us Today." Let us listen to His voice as He speaks.

I. GOD IS SAYING, "CHRIST IS COMING SOON."

I believe God is saying, "O earth, earth, earth, hear the Word of the Lord" (Jer. 22:29). The Word of the Lord declares that Jesus Christ is coming again and many indications are given us today by God that His coming is near. There is the rise of Russia as a world power (Ezek. 38; 39); the revival of Israel (Ezek. 37; Matt. 24:32-34); the ecumenical movement (Rev. 17); the apostasy (II Thess. 2:3; II Tim. 3:1-5); the rise of world government; the U.N.; the Middle East; the alignment of the nations; increase in travel and knowledge (Dan. 12:4); and many others.

J. Dwight Pentecost writes in *Prophecy for Today*, "When you see from all of these great movements how the stage is set so that these events could take place almost overnight, I think there is only one conclusion that a person could make, and that is that the coming of the Lord MUST be drawing nigh. It is my absolute conviction that there is not a single line of prophecy that yet must be fulfilled in order for us to say, 'He can come now.'"

II. GOD IS SAYING, "JUDGMENT IS COMING SOON."

When Christ comes for His own and takes them out of the world, then an awful time of judgment will come upon the world. Jesus spoke about it in Matthew 24:21: "For then shall be great tribulation, such as was not since the beginning of the world to this time, no, nor ever shall be." In this time of judgment, lasting for seven years, over one-half of the world's population will be killed (Rev. 6:8; 9:18), and we read, "And the slain of the Lord shall be at that day from one end of the earth even unto the other end of the earth . . . " (Jer. 25:33). (See also Revelation 6:3-8, 12-17; 8:7-13; 9:1-18; 16:1-21; 19:11-21.)

III. GOD IS SAYING, "BE PREPARED."

God warned, "Prepare to meet thy God . . . " (Amos 4:12), and Jesus commanded, "Therefore be ye also ready: for in such an hour as ye think not the Son of man cometh" (Matt. 24:44). To be prepared, we must have Christ as personal Saviour.

HEAR GOD'S VOICE BEFORE IT'S TOO LATE

I read a tract recently which told of a small iron-working town where the mills are kept running day and night. The steam hammers, some of them several tons in weight, are constantly kept busy, beating out the huge masses of molten iron. The inhabitants of the town had become accustomed to the constant noise, and could sleep soundly through the night without being disturbed.

One night, because of some breakdown in the machinery, these hammers suddenly stopped working, and the consequence was that nearly everyone in this town woke up. What awakened them? Not the oft-repeated stroke of the heavy hammers, but their sudden stopping.

This reminds us of the state of millions of people in our day. While the gospel hammer is kept at work ("Is not my word like as a fire? saith the Lord; and like a hammer . . ." Jer. 23:29), millions within sound of it are fast asleep. But the time will soon come when the Lord Jesus Christ shall return and take His people away, and then the hammer of God's Word shall suddenly cease. Then there shall be an awakening of many gospel-hardened sleepers, but it will be too late for them to be saved (Matt. 25:1-10; Mark 13:35-37). Wake up now and heed God's voice before it's too late.

ARE YOU LISTENING?

Who is going to take the time
　　To listen to the Lord?
To stop your worldly scurrying
　　And heed unto His Word?
God gives to us the WARNING
　　That Christ is coming soon.
Accept the Lord and be prepared.
　　He could come night or noon.
And when the Lord comes back again
　　To take the saved away,
The time is gone — there's no more chance —
　　'Twill be God's Judgment Day.

— Sandra Talkington
(Written after hearing the author's message,
"God Is Saying Something to Us Today")

UNIT XIV
GOD KNOWS

Many times I have heard people say, "God knows." I have searched the Bible to see what "God Knows."

God knows:

I. WHOM HE HAS CHOSEN — John 13:18.

II. HIS SHEEP — John 10:14, 27.

III. THEM THAT TRUST HIM — Nahum 1:7.

IV. THEM THAT ARE HIS — II Timothy 2:19.

V. THE WAY THAT WE TAKE — Job 23:10; Psalm 1:6.

VI. WHAT THINGS WE NEED — Matthew 6:8, 32.

VII. OUR FRAME — Psalm 103:14.

VIII. THE DAYS OF THE UPRIGHT — Psalm 37:18.

IX. WHAT WE ARE — Psalm 139:1.

X. WHAT WE DO — Psalm 139:2a.

XI. WHAT WE THINK — Psalm 139:2b.

XII. ALL OUR WAYS — Psalm 139:3.

XIII. WHAT WE SAY — Psalm 139:4.

XIV. WHERE WE GO — Psalm 139:7-12.

XV. THE HEARTS OF ALL MEN — I Kings 8:39; Psalm 44:21; Luke 16:14; Acts 15:8.

XVI. OUR HYPOCRISY — Mark 12:15.

XVII. THE PROUD — Psalm 138:6.

XVIII. OUR FOOLISHNESS — Psalm 69:5.

XIX. OUR ABODE, OUR GOING OUT, OUR COMING IN, OUR RAGE AGAINST HIM — II Kings 19:27.

XX. OUR WORKS AND THOUGHTS — Isaiah 66:18; Psalm 94:11; Revelation 2:2, 9, 13, 19.

XXI. OUR TRANSGRESSIONS AND SINS — Amos 5:12.

XXII. THE THINGS THAT COME INTO OUR MINDS, EVERY ONE OF THEM — Ezekiel 11:5.

XXIII. WHEN WE DO NOT HAVE THE LOVE OF GOD IN US — John 5:42.

XXIV. ALL THINGS — John 16:30; 21:17; Acts 15:18; I John 3:20.

Surely, we can say with Hannah, "the Lord is a God of knowledge ... (I Sam. 2:3), and exclaim with Paul, "O the depth of the riches both of the wisdom and knowledge of God! how unsearchable are his judgments, and his ways past finding out!" (Rom. 11:33).

God knows you — I trust that you really know Him, because knowing Him is life eternal (John 17:3).

THE LORD KNEW THE WAY SPURGEON SHOULD TAKE

Spurgeon, the Prince of preachers, tells how the Lord led him:

Soon after I had begun to preach the Word in the village of Water-beach, I was strongly advised to enter Stepney, now Regent's Park College, to prepare more fully for the ministry. Knowing that solid learning is never an encumbrance, and is often a great means of usefulness, I felt inclined to avail myself of the opportunity of attaining it: although I hoped that I might be useful without a college training, I decided that I should be more useful with it.

Dr. Angus, the tutor of the college, visited Cambridge, and it was arranged that we should meet at the house of Mr. Macmillan, the publisher. Thinking and praying over the matter, I entered the house exactly at the time appointed, and was shown into a room where I waited patiently a couple of hours, feeling too much impressed with my own insignificance, and the greatness of the tutor from London, to venture to ring the bell, and make enquiries for the long delay.

At last, patience having had her perfect work, and my school engagements requiring me to attend to my duties as an usher, the bell was set in motion, and on the arrival of the servant, the waiting young man was informed that the Doctor had tarried in another room until he could stay no longer, and had gone off to London by train. The stupid girl had given no information to the family that anyone had called, and had been shown into the drawing room; and consequently, the meeting never came about, although designed by both parties. I was not a little disappointed at the moment, but have a thousand times since thanked the Lord very heartily for the strange Providence which forced my steps into another path. The Lord still guides His people by His wisdom, and orders all their paths in love; and in times of perplexity, by ways mysterious and remarkable, He makes them to "hear a voice behind them, saying, 'This is the way, walk ye in it.'"

HE KNOWS!

He knows it all — the winding path, the sky o'ercast and grey,
   The steepness of the mountainside, the roughness of the way;
He knows it all — the haunting fear, the doubtings that distress,
   The wond'rings and perplexities, and all the strain and stress.
He knows it all — each troubled thought, each anxious wave of care,
   And every burden, every grief, or cross that thou dost bear;
He knows it all — be His to choose, and thine to take His choice!
He knows it all! He planned it so! Then trust Him, and rejoice!

                       — E. Margaret Clarkson

UNIT XV
THE GOD-PLANNED LIFE
Ephesians 2:10

One of the greatest discoveries I ever made in my Christian life was that God has a plan for every Christian's life, and that plan can be known and followed. This is according to reason, reality, and revelation. It's reasonable that God who created us and redeemed us would have a plan for us. It's according to reality that many Christians have found and followed God's plan for their lives. And it's according to revelation, because there are many Scripture verses that tell us that God has a plan, or will, for our lives (Ps. 32:8; 37:23; Prov. 3:5, 6; Acts 22:14; Rom. 12:1, 2; Eph. 2:10; 5:17; 6:6; Col. 1:9; 4:12).

The God-planned life is:

I. A SURRENDERED LIFE — Romans 12:1, 2.

In these two verses of Scripture, God shows us three things that will be true of us if we "prove what is that good, and acceptable, and perfect, will of God." The first is found in verse 1: "I beseech you therefore, brethren, by the mercies of God, that ye present your bodies a living sacrifice, holy, acceptable unto God, which is your reasonable service." In order for a Christian to know God's will, he must be surrendered to that will, whatever it may be. That saintly man of God, James H. McConkey, said, "Yield your life to Him by one act of trustful, irrevocable surrender. . . . So shall you come steadily to know and see God's will for your life."

II. A SEPARATED LIFE — Romans 12:2a.

"And be not conformed to this world. . . ." The life that follows God's plan is separated from the world and from worldliness. It is not conformed to the world's pleasures, patterns, or principles, but is being "conformed to the image of his [God's] Son . . ." (Rom. 8:29). The world crucified Christ and a true Christian who lives in the center of God's will obeys the Word of God which says, "Love not the world, neither the things that are in the world. If any man love the world, the love of the Father is not in him" (I John 2:15). (See also John 15:19; 17:14, 16; Gal. 1:4; 6:14; James 4:4; I John 2:16, 17.)

III. A SPIRTUAL LIFE — Romans 12:2b.

"be ye transformed by the renewing of your mind. . . ." God's plans cannot be known and followed by carnally-minded Christians. God only reveals His plan to those who are spiritually-minded and whose lives are being transformed by the Holy Spirit of God.

42

"IT'S JUST LIKE THE PLAN"

You remember the story of the engineer of the Brooklyn bridge. During its building he was injured. For many long months he was shut up in his room. His gifted wife shared his toils, and carried his plans to the workmen. At last the great bridge was completed. Then the invalid architect asked to see it. They put him upon a cot, and carried him to the bridge. They placed him where he could see the magnificent structure in all its beauty. There he lay, in his helplessness, intently scanning the work of his genius. He marked the great cables, the massive piers, the mighty anchorages which fettered it to the earth. His critical eye ran over every beam, every girder, every chord, every rod. He noted every detail carried out precisely as he had dreamed it in his dreams, and wrought it out in his plans and specifications. And then as the joy of achievement filled his soul, as he saw and realized that it was finished exactly as he had designed it; in an ecstasy of delight he cried out: "It's just like the plan, it's just like the plan."

Some day we shall stand in the glory and looking up into His face, cry out: "O God, I thank Thee that Thou didst turn me aside from my wilful and perverse way, to Thy loving and perfect one. I thank Thee that Thou didst ever lead me to yield my humble life to Thee. And now that I see my finished life, no longer 'through a glass darkly' but in the face to face splendor of Thine own glory, I thank Thee, O God, I thank Thee that it's just like the plan; it's just like the plan."

— James H. McConkey

THE GOD-PLANNED LIFE

Why do I drift on a storm-tossed sea,
    With neither compass, nor star, nor chart,
When, as I drift, God's own plan for me,
    Waits at the door of my slow-trusting heart?
Down from the heavens it drops like a scroll,
    Each day a bit will the Master unroll,
Each day a mite of the veil will He lift,
    Why do I falter? Why wander, and drift?
Help me, O God, in the plan to believe:
    Help me my fragment each day to receive,
Oh, that my will may with Thine have no strife!
    God-yielded wills find the God-planned life.

UNIT XVI
"THE GOOD AND THE RIGHT WAY"
I Samuel 12:23, 24

As I was reading my Bible one day, I came to these two verses. In them, God showed me the title of this message in verse 23: "The Good and the Right Way," and in verse 24, He revealed to me a three-point outline of that good and right way.

Here is "The Good and the Right Way":

I. "ONLY FEAR THE LORD" — v. 24a.

A note in the Pilgrim Bible says: "The fear of the Lord is the attitude of heart that the children of God have toward their heavenly Father. While perfectly at home in His presence, and trusting Him reverently, they realize His greatness and stand in awe of Him. Such fear produces a hatred of evil as well as a love of God (Prov. 8:13). It leads to such conduct as will honor the Lord (Prov. 19:23; see also 14:27). It is the beginning of all of man's learning."

The Word of God constantly refers to the "fear of the Lord," and the unsaved are commanded to fear the Lord (Eccles. 8:11-13; Matt. 10:28), as well as the saved (II Cor. 7:1; I Peter 1:17).

II. "SERVE HIM IN TRUTH WITH ALL YOUR HEART" — v. 24b.

Paul wrote, "And whatsoever ye do, do it heartily, as to the Lord, and not unto men; Knowing that of the Lord ye shall receive the reward of the inheritance: for ye serve the Lord Christ" (Col. 3:23, 24).

May we be like Hezekiah, of whom it was said, "And in every work that he began in the service of the house of God, and in the law, and in the commandments, to seek his God, he did it with all his heart, and prospered" (I Chron. 31:21).

III. "CONSIDER HOW GREAT THINGS HE HATH DONE FOR YOU" — v. 24c.

Here is given the motive for fearing the Lord and serving Him in truth with all our heart — the great things He has done for us. If we are saved, God has saved us, He keeps us, He supplies our every need, He gives us peace, He gives us joy, He blesses us with all spiritual blessings, and thank God, one day He will take us to Himself so that we shall be with Him forever (Eph. 2:8, 9; John 10:27-29; 14:27; 15:11; Phil. 4:19; Eph. 1:3; I Thess. 4:16, 17).

Surely, if we would consider all He has done for us, we would fear Him and serve Him in truth with all our heart. This is "The Good and the Right Way."

CHRIST'S SLAVE FOR THE REST OF HER LIFE

A young convert on the west coast of Africa was saved out of the most horrible savagery. One Christmas Day she came into the house of God to offer her sacrifice of praise in the form of a gift on the Lord's birthday.

The congregation was so very, very poor that most of them had only a handful of vegetables to bring, and some only a bunch of flowers to show their goodwill. If anyone would bring a coin worth a penny or two, it was counted a particularly valuable gift. But here came this girl, sixteen years of age and just saved out of paganism, to offer her gift to the Saviour. From under her old dress she drew out and handed to the missionary a silver coin worth about three shillings and six-pence (about $1.00).

The missionary was so amazed at the magnitude of the gift that he refused at first to accept it, for he thought surely she must have gotten it dishonestly. Lest he create confusion, however, he did accept it, but at the close of the service called the girl aside to ask her where she had gotten such a fortune for one in her condition.

She explained to him very simply that in order to give to Christ an offering that satisfied her own heart, she had gone to a neighbouring planter and sold herself to him as a slave for the rest of her life for this three shillings and sixpence. She had now brought the whole financial equivalent of her life of pledged service and laid it down in a single gift at the feet of her Lord!

— Darkness and Light

AFLAME FOR GOD

From prayer that asks that I may be sheltered from winds that beat
    on Thee,
  From fearing when I should aspire, from faltering when I should
      climb higher,
From silken self, O Captain, free Thy soldier who would follow Thee.
From subtle love of softening things, from easy choices, weakenings,
  Not thus are spirits fortified, not this way went the Crucified;
From all that dims Thy Calvary, O Lamb of God, deliver me.
Give me the love that leads the way, the faith that nothing can dismay,
  The hope no disappointments tire, the passion that would burn
      like fire,
Let me not sink to be a clod: make me Thy fuel, Flame of God.

— Amy Carmichael

UNIT XVII
HE'S COUNTING ON US

A. T. Pierson has truthfully said, "Witnessing is the whole work of the whole Church for the whole age." Yes, God is counting on us who belong to Him to tell others about Christ.

I. GOD'S PROGRAM.

God has given us His program to evangelize the world very clearly in Mark 16:15: "Go ye into all the world, and preach the gospel to every creature." He gave a similar commission in Matthew 28:19, 20; Luke 24:47, 48; John 20:21; and Acts 1:8.

J. E. Conant has stated well the program of God for the church: "The Great Commission, therefore, when we sum it up, is a personal command to every Christian to go into every nook and corner of his personal world, and seek, by witnessing in the power of the Holy Spirit to the Good News of God's saving grace through the shed blood of Christ, to win every lost soul in his personal world to salvation."

II. GOD'S PURPOSE.

When God gave the church His program, He had a very definite purpose in view. There are at least two things He had in mind.

A. To Save the Lost.

God is "not willing that any should perish, but that all should come to repentance" (II Peter 3:9), and His desire is that all men be saved and come unto the knowledge of the truth (I Tim. 2:4). The lost are not coming to our churches today, so we must go to them. This is the only program that will reach all of the lost.

B. To Save the Church

When Christians are witnessing to others about Christ they will be saved from backsliding, from selfishness, from worldliness, from drifting, from prayerlessness, from church strife, and from powerlessness.

III. GOD'S POWER.

God's program must have God's power, and He has promised us that in Acts 1:8. God has given every Christian the Holy Spirit and every Christian has been commanded by God to "be filled with the Spirit" (Eph. 5:18). When we are filled with the Holy Spirit, then we can speak the Word of God with boldness and people will be brought to Christ (Acts 4:31; 11:24).

46

"I'M COUNTING ON THEM"

Somebody has supposed the scene that he thinks may have taken place after Jesus went back. The Master is walking down the golden street one day, arm in arm with Gabriel, talking intently, earnestly. Gabriel is saying, "Master, you died for the whole world down there, did you not?"

"Yes."

"You must have suffered much."

"Yes," again comes the answer.

"And do they all know about it?"

"Oh, no! Only a few in Palestine know about it so far."

"Well, Master, what's your plan? What have you done about telling the world that you died for, that you *have* died for them? What's your plan?"

"Well," the Master is supposed to answer, "I asked Peter, and James and John, and Andrew, and some more of them down there just to make it the business of their lives to tell others, and the others are to tell others, and the others others, and yet others, and still others, until the last man in the farthest circle has heard the story and has felt the thrilling and the thralling power of it."

"Yes — but — suppose Peter fails. Suppose after a while John simply does not tell others. Suppose their descendants, their successors away off in the . . . twentieth century, get so busy about things — some of them proper enough, some maybe not quite so proper — that they do not tell others — what then?"

And back comes that quiet wondrous voice of Jesus, "Gabriel, I haven't made any other plans — I'm counting on them."

— S. D. Gordon

HIS PLAN

There's only one way that this lost world can know
    That Jesus for sinners hath died;
To spread the glad tidings He's bidden us go,
    And no other way doth provide.
He's counting on us the story to tell,
    His scheme of redemption for man;
He's counting on you; He's counting on me.
    The Master has no other plan.

— Mrs. C. H. Morris

UNIT XVIII
HOW ABOUT YOUR HEART?

This is the title of a song I sing frequently in my evangelistic meetings. God says much about the heart in the Bible. He tries the heart (I Chron. 29:17; Jer. 10:3); knows the heart (Ps. 44:21); searches the heart (I Chron. 28:9; Jer. 17:10); ponders the heart (Prov. 21:2; 24:12); understands the thoughts of the heart (I Chron. 28:9); opens the heart (Acts 16:14); and establishes the heart (I Thess. 3:13).

How about Your Heart? God searches the heart (Jer. 17:10). As He searches your heart, does He find:

I. A TREASURY OF EVIL? — Genesis 6:5; Ecclesiastes 8:11; 9:3; Jeremiah 17:9; Matthew 12:35b; Mark 7:21-23.
A TREASURY OF GOOD? — Psalm 40:8; 119:11; Jeremiah 32:40; Matthew 12:35a.

II. A HARD HEART? — Proverbs 29:1; Zechariah 7:11, 12; Mark 3:5; Hebrews 3:7, 8, 15; 4:7.
A SOFT HEART? — II Kings 22:19; Job 23:16; Acts 16:14.

III. A FOOLISH HEART? — Proverbs 12:23; Romans 1:21.
A WISE HEART? — Proverbs 10:8; 14:33.

IV. AN UNBELIEVING HEART? — Hebrews 3:12.
A BELIEVING HEART? — Proverbs 3:5, 6; Romans 10:9, 10.

V. A DOUBLE HEART? — Psalm 12:2; Hosea 10:2; Matthew 6:24.
A SINGLE HEART? — I Samuel 12:24; II Chronicles 16:9a; Acts 2:46; Ephesians 6:5, 6; Colossians 3:22.

VI. A PROUD HEART? — Psalm 101:5.
AN HUMBLE HEART? — Psalm 34:18; Isaiah 57:15.

VII. A HEART INFLUENCED BY THE DEVIL? — John 13:2; Acts 5:3.
A HEART INFLUENCED BY THE LORD? — Psalm 27:14; Proverbs 21:1; Jeremiah 20:9.

For many people, the answer to the question asked by Jehu, "Is thine heart right . . . ?" (II Kings 10:15) would be ". . . thy heart is not right in the sight of God" (Acts 8:21). If that is your answer, thank God, through repentance toward God and faith toward our Lord Jesus Christ (Acts 20:21), God will touch your heart (I Sam. 10:26), and say to you, "A new heart also will I give you . . ." (Ezek. 36:26).

"DADDY, DADDY, FEEL YOUR HEART"

Harry Ironside, in "Addresses on the Gospel of John," tells this interesting story:

I was talking to a small group of boys and girls in a Sunday School in San Francisco. "How sad to know, each time you say 'No' to the Lord Jesus, your heart gets a little harder, and if you keep on saying 'No,' the heart gets harder and harder until by-and-by God calls it a heart of stone, and you persist in spurning His grace, and you will therefore die in your sins." So I was pleading with those boys and girls to give their hearts to Jesus in their early days. There was one dear little tot there, only five years old. Her mother brought her to Sunday School and then took her home. The little one was thinking of her own dear father who never went to hear the Word of God. When she got to the house she darted into her father's arms, and said, "Daddy, Daddy, feel your heart! Is it getting like stone?" He said, "What are you talking about?" She said, "Well, the man at Sunday School said if you say 'No' to Jesus you are going to get a stone inside. Oh, Daddy, I hope you haven't, for if you have, you can't be saved." The father said angrily to the mother, "What have they been telling this child, anyway?" Then the mother explained a little more fully, and when he saw the tears in his wife's eyes and felt the arms of his little girl about his neck, and heard her saying, "Oh, Daddy, don't go on saying 'No' to Jesus," he looked up and said, "Well I think I had better settle this thing," and he got down on his knees and yielded his life to Christ.

IS THY HEART RIGHT WITH GOD?

Have thy affections been nailed to the cross? Is thy heart right with God?
　Countest thou all things for Jesus but loss? Is thy heart right with God?
Hast thou dominion o'er self and o'er sin? Is thy heart right with God?
　Over all evil without and within? Is thy heart right with God?
Is there no more condemnation for sin? Is thy heart right with God?
　Does Jesus rule in the temple within? Is thy heart right with God?
Are all thy pow'rs under Jesus' control? Is thy heart right with God?
　Does He each moment abide in thy soul? Is thy heart right with God?
Is thy heart right with God, washed in the crimson flood,
　Cleansed and made holy, humble, and lowly, right in the sight of God?

— Rev. Elisha A. Hoffman

UNIT XIX
HOW A PERSON IS LIKE A MULE
Mark 11:1-10

God's Word says in Job 11:12, "For vain man would be wise, though man be born like a wild ass's colt." In the Scripture passage above, we find seven ways as to "How a Person Is Like a Mule."

I. HE IS TIED — v. 4.

The colt was "tied," and so is a person in sin: "His own iniquities shall take the wicked himself, and he shall be holden with the cords of his sins" (Prov. 5:22). (See also II Tim. 2:26.)

II. HE IS "BY THE DOOR"— v. 4.

Jesus Christ said, "I am the door . . . " (John 10:9). Jesus Christ is near us — "though he be not far from every one of us" (Acts 17:27); "Behold, I stand at the door and knock . . . " (Rev. 3:20).

III. HE IS "WITHOUT" — v. 4.

The unsaved person is without Christ and God (Eph. 2:12); without understanding (Rom. 1:31); without strength (Rom. 5:6); without light (John 8:12); without life (John 14:6); without peace (Isa. 57:20, 21); without rest (Matt. 11:28); without salvation (Acts 4:12); without hope (Eph. 2:12); without all spiritual blessings (Eph. 1:3); and without Heaven (John 14:1-6).

IV. HE IS AT THE CROSSROADS — "in a place where two ways met . . . " — v. 4.

Jesus Christ spoke of the two ways — the broad way and the narrow way in Matthew 7:13, 14. The unsaved person has to make a choice as to which way he shall choose: "I have set before you life and death, blessing and cursing: therefore choose life" (Deut. 30:19; Josh. 24:15).

V. HE NEEDS TO BE LOOSED — ". . . and they loose him" — v. 4.

When a person receives Jesus Christ as personal Saviour and Lord, he can say with the Apostle John: "To him who ever loves us and has once [for all] loosed and freed us from our sins by his own blood" (Rev. 1:5 A.N.T.).

VI. HE IS NEEDED BY THE LORD — ". . . the Lord hath need of him . . . " — v. 3.

He needs us who are saved to tell others until the whole world has heard the gospel (Mark 16:15).

VII. HE CAN BE USED TO TAKE THE LORD TO THE MULTITUDES — vv. 7-9.

After a person is saved, the Lord can use him as a witness unto Jesus Christ "unto the uttermost part of the earth" (Acts 1:8; Matt. 9:36-38).

50

"THE LORD HATH NEED OF HIM"

Henry G. Bosch related this interesting story in *Our Daily Bread*: Note how the disciples sought a little colt for an important assignment! Jesus, the Son of God, was to make His triumphal entry into Jerusalem on this lowly beast. It therefore became more significant than the thousands of similar animals in the land of Palestine simply because the Lord had "need of him!"

Many years ago in Scotland a faithful minister was criticized by one of his board members. "There must be something wrong with your preaching and work," said the deacon, "for there has been only one person added to the church in the past year, and he is only a boy!" The old minister went into the pulpit grieved and crushed. Later he lingered in the church to pray. After being on his knees for a while he became conscious of the fact that he was not alone. Looking up he saw it was "only a boy." "Well, Robert," said the preacher, "what is it?" "Please, Pastor, do you think if I were willing to work hard for an education I could ever become a preacher — or perhaps a missionary?" Tears filled the eyes of the minister. At length he said, "This heals the ache in my heart, Robert. I see the Divine Hand now. Yes, I think you will become a great preacher." He was "only a boy," but Robert grew up to be a mighty servant of God. Indeed, the measure of the old minister's reward may well be found in the gathered fruitage of the labors of that world-renowned African missionary — Robert Moffat!

"Just a colt," and "just a boy," but very significant — because the Lord had need of them!

WRAPPED IN SELF

Wrapped in himself he comes to church, takes off his overcoat and hat,
   And, going to his pew, sits down, pulling his problem tighter around
      his shoulder,
Crawling . . . cold . . . deeper into himself as the hymns, the anthems,
   the prayers,
And the sermon pour over him.
Then wrapped in himself, his overcoat and hat, he goes away again,
   Wondering vaguely where God was during the service and how he
      missed Him.
As though he expected to find God in his pocket,
   Or gazing out between the hands of his watch, or rolled up in the
      service leaflet.
Without God in his pocket or in his soul, he goes away . . .
   Wrapped in himself.

— Bob Carlin

UNIT XX
"HOW GREAT THOU ART"

The song, "How Great Thou Art," has become one of the best-known and best-loved songs in recent years. With Jeremiah, the prophet, we exclaim, "Forasmuch as there is none like unto thee, O Lord; thou art great, and thy name is great in might" (Jer. 10:6).

I. GOD IS GREAT IN POWER — Psalm 147:5; Jeremiah 32:17-19; Nahum 1:3.

We can say thankfully, "there is nothing too hard for thee" (Jer. 32:17).

II. GOD IS GREAT IN WORKS — Psalm 92:5; 111:2.

"Great and marvelous are thy works, Lord God Almighty . . . " (Rev. 15:3).

III. GOD IS GREAT IN GOODNESS — Psalm 31:19; 33:5; 34:8; 65:11.

"The Lord is good to all . . . " (Ps. 145:9).

IV. GOD IS GREAT IN MERCY — Psalm 57:10; 86:13; 103:11; 117:2; 119:156; 145:8.

Thank God, "his mercy endureth for ever" (Ps. 136:1-26).

V. GOD IS GREAT IN LOVE — Ephesians 2:4; John 3:16; Romans 5:8; 8:38, 39; I John 3:1.

> "O love of God, how rich and pure,
> How measureless and strong;
> It shall forever more endure,
> The saints' and angels' song."
> — F. M. Lehman

VI. GOD IS GREAT IN SALVATION — Hebrews 2:3; 5:9.

God says, "my salvation shall be for ever, and my righteousness shall not be abolished" (Isa. 51:6).

VII. GOD IS GREAT IN WRATH — Zechariah 7:12; Revelation 6:16, 17; 14:19; 20:11-15; 21:8.

When God's great power, works, goodness, mercy, love, and salvation are rejected or neglected, then people will have to experience His great wrath. If you have never done it, put your complete trust in our "great" Saviour (Luke 1:31, 32) and then you too can say, "For thou art great, and doest wondrous things: thou art God alone" (Ps. 86:10).

GOD IS GREAT IN LOVE

Recently I read of a man in Florida who operated a huge draw-bridge over a large river. He would lift the bridge to let the boats go through and then lower it back in place for the trains to cross the river. One day, a boat blew its horn for him to lift the bridge, which he did. It was only twelve minutes before a large passenger train was due with over three hundred passengers on it. The train was running one hundred miles an hour, and there was no way to flag it down. After the boat had gone under the bridge, the operator saw his five-year old son sitting on top of the great cogs that raised the bridge up and down. There was no way in the world for him to get his son off and get the bridge down in time for the train to cross in safety. The man cried with a bitter cry, turned his head, and pushed the button for the bridge to be lowered. The bridge barely got in place when the train came dashing across. The man went where his son was and found him ground to pieces beyond recognition, every bone crushed.

This man had two choices. One, to let his son live and the people die, or, let his son die and the people live. He chose the latter. God looked down on this earth and found man sinning and living for the devil. He had to let His Son die for them or let them go to hell and the lake of fire. So God let His Son die to save everyone who would trust Him.

MY GOD, HOW WONDERFUL THOU ART!

My God, how wonderful Thou art,
   Thy majesty how bright!
How beautiful Thy Mercy-seat
   In depths of burning light!
Yet, I may love Thee, too, O Lord!
   Almighty as Thou art;
For Thou hast stopped to ask of me
   The love of my poor heart.
No earthly father loves like Thee,
   No mother e'er so mild,
Bears and forbears as Thou hast done
   With me, Thy sinful child.
My God, how wonderful Thou art,
   Thou everlasting Friend!
On Thee I'll stay my trusting heart
   Till faith in vision end.

UNIT XXI
"I KNOW THAT MY REDEEMER LIVETH"
Job 19:25

This verse was the favorite of Jenny Lind, the Swedish Nightingale. The words are inscribed on her tomb at Great Malvern Cemetery. It is a favorite verse of mine too. "I Know That My Redeemer Liveth":

I. BECAUSE HE SAID HE WOULD RISE FROM THE DEAD.
(Matt. 16:21; Mark 8:31; Luke 9:22; John 2:19-21).

II. BECAUSE OF THE EMPTY TOMB.
(Matt. 28:1-6; Mark 16:1-6; Luke 24:1-6; John 20:1-13).

III. BECAUSE OF THOSE WHO SAW HIM AFTER HE AROSE.
Acts 1:3: Mary Magdalene (Mark 16:9-11); other women (Matthew 28:8-10); Peter (Luke 24:34); Emmaus disciples (Luke 24:13-15); ten apostles (John 20:19-24); eleven apostles (John 20:26); seven apostles at Sea of Galilee (John 21:1, 2); eleven apostles in Galilee (Matt. 28:16, 17); more than 500 brethren (I Cor. 15:6); James (I Cor. 15:7); Paul (I Cor. 15:8); Stephen (Acts 7:55-60); John (Rev. 1:10-19).

IV. BECAUSE OF THE CHANGE IN HIS DISCIPLES AFTER HE AROSE.
Before His resurrection, His disciples were timid and fearful, but after His resurrection they were bold and fearless (compare John 20:19; Acts 4:29-33).

V. BECAUSE OF THE CHANGE FROM THE JEWISH SABBATH TO THE LORD'S DAY.
Jesus arose on the first day of the week. The Jewish Sabbath was on the seventh day of the week. The early church of Jewish believers met for worship on the Lord's Day, the first day of the week, instead of the seventh, in commemoration of Jesus' resurrection (Acts 20:7).

VI. BECAUSE OF THE CHRISTIAN CHURCH.
The Christian Church was established by Jesus Christ and its members love, honor, and worship Him (Matt. 16:18).

VII. BECAUSE HE LIVES WITHIN MY HEART.
I can say with Paul, "Christ liveth in me..." (Gal. 2:20), and He has changed my life completely. Thank God, I can truthfully say that I am "a new creation: old things are passed away; behold all things are become new" (II Cor. 5:17).

"HE LIVES!"

"Why should I worship a dead Jew?"

This was the question asked the Reverend A. H. Ackley by a young Jew who had attended evangelistic services for five or six successive nights where Mr. Ackley had been preaching. This young man had remained at the close of the service and Mr. Ackley had tried to persuade him to receive Jesus Christ as his personal Saviour and Lord when this question was asked.

Mr. Ackley was shocked by the question, and said to his questioner, "He lives! I tell you, He is not dead, but lives here and now! Jesus Christ is more alive today than ever before. I can prove it by my own experience, as well as the testimony of countless thousands." As he continued speaking to the Jewish man, he had the privilege of winning him to Jesus Christ. He was always alert to suggestions for sermons and songs, and this experience led him to write the very popular song, "He Lives." He said, "The thought of His ever living presence brought the music promptly and easily. The words followed immediately."

MY REDEEMER LIVES

I know that my Redeemer lives;
　　What joy the blest assurance gives!
He lives, He lives, who once was dead;
　　He lives, my everlasting Head!

He lives, to bless me with His love;
　　He lives, to plead for me above;
He lives, my hungry soul to feed;
　　He lives, to help in time of need.

He lives, to grant me daily breath;
　　He lives, and I shall conquer death;
He lives, my mansion to prepare;
　　He lives, to bring me safely there.

He lives, all glory to His name;
　　He lives, my Saviour, still the same —
What joy the blest assurance gives,
　　I know that my Redeemer lives!

　　　　　　　　— Samuel Medley

UNIT XXII
I'M THANKFUL
I Timothy 1:12

According to the Bible, we should be thankful for: the supply of our material needs (I Tim. 4:3-5); the goodness and mercy of God (Ps. 106:1); victory over death and the grave (I Cor. 15:57); the triumph of the Gospel (II Cor. 2:14); the conversion of others (Rom. 6:17); all men (I Tim. 2:1); all things (Eph. 5:20).

In this message, I wish to give my testimony in the words of Paul's testimony found in our text.

I. I'M THANKFUL FOR THE SAVIOUR — "And I *thank Christ Jesus our Lord....*"

Paul was thankful for the Lord Jesus Christ, our Saviour and cries out in II Corinthians 9:15: "Thanks be unto God for his unspeakable gift," or, as the *Amplified New Testament* renders it: 'Now thanks be to God for His gift [precious] beyond telling — His indescribable, free Gift." I'm thankful that:

> Living, He loved me; dying, He saved me;
> Buried, He carried my sins far away;
> Rising, He justified freely forever:
> One day He's coming — oh, glorious day!
>
> — J. Wilbur Chapman

II. I'M THANKFUL FOR STRENGTH — "who hath enabled me ...," which means "to empower" or "increase in strength." Paul used this verb in Philippians 4:13: "*I have strength* for all things in Christ Who empowers me — I am ready for anything and equal to anything through *Him Who infuses inner strength into me,* [that is, I am self-sufficient in Christ's sufficiency"]" (A.N.T.). I'm thankful that it's possible to "*be strong in the Lord,* and in the power of his might" (Eph. 6:10), and God promises, "as thy days, *so shall thy strength be*" (Deut. 33:25).

III. I'M THANKFUL FOR SERVICE — "for that he counted me faithful, putting me into the ministry." The word "ministry" means "service," or "ministering." I'm thankful that I have been put into the ministry and for about twenty years I have had the blessed privilege of serving the Lord in many states in this country and in foreign countries. I pray that you and I may "*serve him in truth with all [our] heart* ..." (I Sam. 12:24), and be like David, of whom it is said, that he "*served his own generation by the will of God* ..." (Acts 13:36).

56

SOPHIE FORGOT TO BE THANKFUL

Sophie, the scrubwoman, a German Christian who was used greatly by the Lord, relates this story:

"In the morning I always get down the Bible. I call it my love-letter from Father. Sometimes He scolds a little in the letter; but it vas for 'reproof and correction'; und we need that sometimes. Well this mornink I open to the prayer, 'Our Father which vas in Heaven,' und I says, 'Oh, Father! I know that by heart; gif me something else. That mornink I haf no money to get the coffee and roll; but I did not worry. I thought I gets my breakfast where I was to work; but they vas all through when got there. 'Well,' I say, 'nefer mind, I wait till dinner.' Before dinner the woman goes out und forgets all about me; so no dinner. I got through early, und I vas so hungry I go home ready to cry, und I say, 'Father, how is this; You say You nefer leave me; but I work all day without anything to eat?' Und I began to complain. 'Look here, Sophie,' said Father, almost speaking to my soul plain. 'Look here; this mornink you read in My Book, und when you comes to the prayer where it says, "Gif me this day my daily bread," you don't read it; you say, "Gif me something fresh." Is that stale? Because every day these things come *you forget to be thankful.*' At once I see where I sin, und gets down and say, 'Father, forgive me, gif me this day my daily bread, for Thy child is hungry.'

"When I got off my knees there came a knock, und my landlady vas there with a cup of coffee und some biscuits. She said, 'I thought you were tired, und might not like to get supper; so I brought these in.' Then I thank Father, und begin to shout."

MY THANKSGIVING

For food upon my table, Lord, for clothes that I may wear,
   For shelter of my little home, for all the comforts there;
For health to do my daily tasks, for eyes that I may see;
   For ears to hear the songs of joy, dear Lord, I now thank Thee.
For light that brightens every day and peaceful rest at night,
   For "still small voice" that helps me choose between the wrong and right.
For fellowship of many friends and neighbors kind and true;
   For trees and flowers, birds and bees, and skies above of blue.
I could not all my blessings count, I have so vast a store,
   Each day I am more thankful, Lord, than e'er I was before.
For Christ my loving Saviour dear, throughout eternity,
   My grateful heart shall sing its praise and offer thanks to Thee!

UNIT XXIII
"IN TIMES LIKE THESE"

Ruth Caye Jones has written a beautiful and much-used song, "In Times Like These." These are "perilous times" (II Tim. 3:1), "the latter times" (I Tim. 4:1), the last days of the age before Christ comes again, and we need to have an "...understanding of the times..." (I Chron. 12:32). In this message,, I want to take four thoughts from this well-known song: "you need a Saviour," "you need an anchor," "you need the Bible," and "be not idle."

I. IN TIMES LIKE THESE, YOU NEED A SAVIOUR.

A. Because you are a sinner (Rom. 3:23).

B. Because you are lost (II Cor. 4:3, 4).

C. Because you are under God's condemnation and wrath (John 3:18, 36).

D. Because you are dead in sins (Eph. 2:1).

E. Because you are on your way to Hell (Matt. 10:28; 25:46).

F. Thank God, a Saviour has been provided (Isa. 53:3, 6; Luke 19:10; II Cor. 5:21; I Peter 2:24; 3:18).

G. He must be received (John 1:12; Acts 16:30, 31; Rom. 10:9, 13; II Cor. 6:2).

II. IN TIMES LIKE THESE, YOU NEED SECURITY.

The song says, "You need an anchor," which means anything steady or secure. Thank God, we have an anchor (Heb. 6:17-20), and security (Ps. 46:1-3; Rom. 8:35-39; II Tim. 1:12), if we have Jesus Christ as our personal Saviour.

III. IN TIMES LIKE THESE, YOU NEED THE SCRIPTURES.

The words of the song say, "You need the Bible." We have been told concerning the Bible to:

A. Know it in your head (II Tim. 2:15).

B. Stow it in your heart (Prov. 4:4).

C. Show it in your life (John 13:17; James 1:22).

D. Sow it in the world (Ps. 126:5, 6; Luke 8:5, 11).

We can be thankful the Scriptures are available.

IV. IN TIMES LIKE THESE, YOU NEED SERVICE.

Mrs. Jones has written, "O be not idle." Surely, in the light of the soon return of Jesus Christ, we should be serving the Lord in truth with all of our hearts (I Sam. 12:24; Col. 3:23, 24). John F. Walvoord writes, "Now is the time for Christians to face the task of evangelism, prayer, devotion, and service. All of these are pressed upon us urgently by our present world situation."

THE MAN WHO LOVES THE BIBLE

"In Times Like These You Need the Bible."

There is a man living in a suburb of Kansas City who lost both hands in a premature explosion while blasting stone. His face was much torn. The surgeons did all they could for him — but his eyesight was utterly destroyed. He had been converted only a year or two. The Bible was his delight, and his distress at no longer being able to read it was great. He chanced to hear of a lady in England who read the Braille type with her lips. Some friends ordered parts of the Bible in the Moon raised type for him and he could hardly wait till they arrived.

But alas! the explosion had destroyed the nerves of his lips — there was no sense of touch there! He wept over the Book and stooped to kiss it farewell, when he happened to touch it with his tongue. His teacher was recalled, and he quickly learned to read the raised characters by running his tongue along them.

"I have read the whole Bible through four times," said he, "and many of the books of the Bible over and over again."

That man loved God's Word.

TIME TO REAP

Now is the time to rise and reap, the fields are harvest white;
    This is the hour, I now repeat, to spread the Gospel light.
This is the hour to give and work until the war is won;
    Oh, let us not our duty shirk before the work is done.
The entire world is Christ's domain, yet heathen millions wait;
    Let's quickly reap that golden grain before it is too late.
We must not let that harvest field grow ripe, then rot and die;
    Oh, let us then the sickle wield, we dare not pass them by.
Our hearts must heed their strong appeals; perhaps our worst defect,
    Is damning souls while we just sit; it's murder by neglect.
It's time to call a halt, dear friend, it's time to pray and weep;
    The sheaves must quickly be brought in; it's time for us to reap!

— Fred D. Jarvis

UNIT XXIV
THE LAST WORDS OF THE RISEN SAVIOUR

Every year, during the week preceding Easter, pastors throughout this country and the world preach a series of messages with this or a similar title: "The Last Words of the Suffering Saviour." In this message I want to call to your attention "The Last Words of the Risen Saviour." Thank God, Christ is alive forevermore and He still speaks to us today.

I. THE RISEN SAVIOUR'S LAST WORDS TO HIS CHURCH BEFORE HE ASCENDED — Matthew 28:18-20.

A. He spoke of His power — v. 18.

B. He spoke of His program — vv. 19, 20a.

1. Make disciples — "Go ye therefore, and teach" ("make disciples of all the nations" — A.N.T.).

2. Baptize them — "baptizing them in the name of the Father, and of the Son, and of the Holy Ghost."

3. Teach them to observe (obey) Jesus' commandments — "Teaching them to observe all things whatsoever I have commanded you. . . ."

C. He spoke of His presence — "I am with you alway, even unto the end of the world" — v. 20b.

May the church of Jesus Christ hear His voice and be filled with His power, fulfill His program, and feel His presence.

II. THE RISEN SAVIOUR'S LAST WORDS TO THE CHURCH AFTER HE ASCENDED — Revelation 2; 3.

A. "I know thy works" (Rev. 2:2, 9, 13, 19; 3:1, 8, 15).

B. "He that hath an ear, let Him hear what the Spirit saith unto the churches" (Rev. 2:7, 11, 17, 29; 3:6, 13, 22).

C. "Repent" (Rev. 2:5, 16, 22; 3:3, 19).

May the churches of today realize that Christ knows our works, may they hear what the Spirit of God is saying to them, and may they repent.

III. THE RISEN SAVIOUR'S LAST WORDS TO EVERYONE — Revelation 22:16-20.

A. His last invitation (v. 17).

B. His last warning (vv. 18, 19).

C. His last promise (v. 20). "Surely, I come quickly." (See also Rev. 22:7, 12.)

May everyone respond to His last invitation, reflect upon His last warning, and rejoice in His last promise.

THE EMPOWERING THOUGHT OF THE LORD'S RETURN

Jack MacArthur speaks of the power of the truth of the Lord's second coming in men's lives:

I was so intrigued with the empowering thought of the Lord's RETURN, so I investigated the lives of men who have been mightily used of God, to find out what they had to say concerning this blessed truth. D. L. Moody was asked the secret of his power and intensity. He said, "I preached for years with the thought that before every sermon was finished the LORD MIGHT COME." J. Wilbur Chapman said, "I preach the Lord's return because the thought of His second coming has changed my whole ministry. I have not the slightest doubt but that we are approaching the last days." (Oh, if it were true then, how much more so it must be now!) G. Campbell Morgan, who just recently left this vale of tears to be with our wonderful Lord, said, speaking in those dark terrible days of the bombing of England, "To me the second coming is the perpetual light of my pathway, making the present bearable. I never lay my head on my pillow without thinking that before morning breaks the final morning may have dawned." Hudson Taylor, that great pioneer for God who tackled the seemingly impossible in China and wrought such mighty things for Christ, said, "This truth of the Lord's return has been the greatest spur to me in missionary service." R. A. Torrey, peerless preacher of yesterday, said, "The truth of our Lord's return is the most precious truth the Bible contains. It fills the heart of a believer with joy. It girds him with strength for the battle. It lifts him above the sorrows and the fears and necessities and trials and ambitions and greed of this world, and makes him in all things more than a conqueror."

HIS WORD STILL STANDS

If you should wake some dreadful day before His throne, and hear
  Him say:
"I am the Way you did not take, although I died once for your
  sake;
I am the Truth you did not heed, you were so sure you had no need;
  I am the Light you did not see — now, darkness for eternity!"
You cannot say, "I did not know"; He plainly wrote and told you so.
  And if you would not read His Word? That Word still stands, "Thus
  saith the Lord!"

                  — Martha Snell Nicholson

UNIT XXV
LIFE, LIBERTY, AND THE PURSUIT OF HAPPINESS

The Declaration of Independence, United States, a document proclaiming the independence of the thirteen English colonies in America, was adopted by the Continental Congress on July 4, 1776. In it are these words: "We hold these truths to be self-evident, that all men are created equal, that they are endowed by their Creator with certain unalienable rights, that among these are Life, Liberty, and the Pursuit of Happiness." It is true that God wants all of us to have these three wonderful gifts.

I. GOD OFFERS US LIFE.

A. He offers us everlasting life (John 3:16; 5:24; 10:27-29; Rom. 6:23; I John 5:11-13).

B. He offers us abundant life (John 10:10).

For this abundant life God gives: abundant grace (Rom. 5:17); abundant pardon (Isa. 55:7); abundant peace (Ps. 37:11); abundant joy (II Cor. 8:2); abundant satisfaction (Ps. 36:8); abundant power (Eph. 3:20); and eventually, an abundant entrance (II Peter 1:11).

II. GOD OFFERS US LIBERTY.

Jesus Christ was sent into the world " . . . to proclaim liberty to the captives . . ." (Isa. 61:1). We are all captives, servants of sin, before Christ sets us free (John 8:34, 36), but thank God, when we trust Christ as our personal Saviour and Lord, we can say, "Christ hath made us free . . ." (Gal. 5:1). We are free from: sin (Rom. 6:18, 22; 8:2); Satan (II Tim. 2:26; Heb. 2:14, 15); and self (Gal. 5:16, 24, 25).

III. GOD OFFERS US HAPPINESS.

"Whoso trusteth in the Lord, happy is he" (Prov. 16:20). Jesus said, "If ye know these things, happy are ye if ye do them" (John 13:17).

> "Trust and obey, for there's no other way
> To be happy in Jesus, but to trust and obey."
>
> — J. H. Sammis

A MILLIONAIRE AND A CATERPILLAR

Herrmann G. Braunlin tells this story:

Like many another man, Titus Salt, a factory boy in England, began life poor. A hard worker, with an inventive mind, he developed a process for using coarse Russian wool and became one of the wealthiest woolen manufacturers. After he invented "alpaca," he became a multi-millionaire. Because his progressive ideas had benefited the whole industrial life of England, Queen Victoria made him a baron.

Was Sir Titus Salt satisfied? He was not.

One Sunday Sir Titus heard a preacher tell about how, while sitting in his garden, he had watched a caterpillar climb a painted stick which had been stuck into the ground as a decoration. The caterpillar slowly climbed to the top of the stick, then reared itself, feeling this way and that for some juicy twig on which to feed, or for some way to further progress. But the caterpillar was disappointed. Groping about, it found nothing. Slowly it returned to the ground, crawling along until it reached another painted stick, and did the same thing all over again. This happened several times.

"There are many painted sticks in the world," said the preacher. "There are the painted sticks of pleasure, of wealth, of power, of fame. All these call to men and say 'Climb me and you will find the desire of your heart; climb me and you will fulfill the purpose of your existence; climb me and taste the fruits of success; climb me and find satisfaction.' But," continued the preacher, "they are only painted sticks."

The very next day the preacher had a visitor. It was the wealthy Baron, who said, "Sir, I was in your congregation last night and heard what you said about the painted sticks. I want to tell you that I have been climbing them, and today I am a weary man. Tell me, is there rest for someone like me?"

The preacher had the great joy of pointing that sin-burdened soul to the One who once said, "Come unto me, all ye that labor and are heavy laden, and I will give you rest" (Matt. 11:28).

NONE BUT CHRIST CAN SATISFY

O Christ, in Thee my soul hath found, and found in Thee alone,
The peace, the joy I sought so long, the bliss till now unknown.
Now, none but Christ can satisfy, none other Name for me;
There's love, and life, and lasting joy, Lord Jesus, found in Thee!

UNIT XXVI
MY FAVORITE MOTTO

Shortly after God saved me, my mother gave me a small wall plaque on which was written: "Only one life, 'twill soon be past; only what's done for Christ will last." These words have been my favorite motto ever since. This motto tells me three things about my life, and yours.

I. "ONLY ONE LIFE" — IT'S SINGLE.

Adoniram Judson once said, "You have but one life in which to prepare for eternity. Had you four or five lives, two or three of them might be spent in carelessness. But you have only one. Every action of that one life gives coloring to your eternity. How important, then, that you spend that life so as to please the Saviour."

II. "'TWILL SOON BE PAST" — IT'S SHORT.

God's Word compares our lives to: a vapor (James 4:14); a flower (Job 14:2; Isa. 40:6; Ps. 103:15); a shadow (Job 14:2; Ps. 102:11; 144:4); a tale that is told (Ps. 90:9); grass (Isa. 40:6; Ps. 90:5; 103:15); a wind that passeth (Ps. 78:39; Job 7:7); a weaver's shuttle (Job 7:6; Isa. 38:12); a shepherd's tent (Isa. 38:12); and foam on the water (Hos. 10:7).

III. "ONLY WHAT'S DONE FOR CHRIST WILL LAST" — IT'S SERIOUS.

As Maltbie D. Babcock has written, "We are not here to play, to dream, to drift. We have hard work to do, and loads to lift."

God's Word tells us that we have been created for His glory (Isa. 43:7), and further tells us, "Whether therefore ye eat, or drink, or whatsoever ye do, do all to the glory of God" (I Cor. 10:13). God has put us on this earth to glorify Him, love Him, fellowship with Him, and serve Him, and we can only do this when we have trusted Jesus Christ as our own personal Saviour and Lord and let Him guide and rule our lives. When we come to the end of our short lives and face eternity, the important thing then will be what we have allowed Him to do in us and through us. Crowley wisely said, "Time is lent to us to be laid out in God's service.... It is precious, short, passing, uncertain, irrevocable when gone, and that for which we must be accountable."

Paul said, "For to me to live is Christ, and to die is gain" (Phil. 1:21). If you can't truthfully say this, my prayer is that you think right now about your life — it's single, short and serious. As Moody said, "Give your life to God. He can do more with it than you can."

"LORD JESUS, LIVE YOUR LIFE IN ME"

Stephen F. Olford, Pastor of Calvary Baptist Church in New York City, relates how he was influenced by the motto "Only One Life":

My parents were missionaries in Angolo, and I was born in Africa. At an early age I was saved. Then the day came when I went to Britain to study to be an engineer. Little by little I lost the glow of my Christian faith.

One night I had a motorcycle accident, was taken to a hospital, where the doctors held out little hope for my recovery. At this time my father was still in Africa and did not know what I was going through. One day I received a letter from him, in which he said, "My son, of most importance is this fact: 'Only one life, 'twill soon be past; only what's done for Christ will last.' " It was like a hammer blow. I was shattered. I could see my life before my Maker as a shrivelled-up piece of wastage.

With father's words echoing in my soul, I capitulated. I just looked into the face of my Lord by faith and said, "I give in. No more rebellion. I have been a fool. I have tried to run my own life and have made an awful mess of it. I want to come back to you. I want You to receive me. I return in humility and in repentance."

As I knelt in the presence of God, a wonderful peace came into my heart. I yielded my life to Him. I said, "Lord Jesus, I want You to take over the reins of my life. I want You to be supreme Sovereign."

And He did it! Not only did God meet me in my deep spiritual need, but He also healed me, for in three weeks' time I was on my feet again.

ONLY ONE LIFE

Two little lines I heard one day as I plodded on in my usual way:
  And they rang in my ears again, and again, repeating in solemn, sweet refrain:
"Only one life, 'twill soon be past; only what's done for Christ will last."
  "Only One life," the still small voice gently allures to the better choice,
Bidding me never let selfish aims overshadow my Saviour's claims.
  Give me, Saviour, a purpose deep, in joy or sorrow Thy trust to keep;
And so thru trouble, care and strife, glorify Thee in my daily life!
  "Only one life, 'twill soon be past; only what's done for Christ will last."

— Christian Graphic

UNIT XXVII
THE OBEDIENT LIFE

A. W. Tozer discerningly says, "To obey, in New Testament usage, means to give earnest attention to the Word, to submit to its authority, and to carry out its instructions. Obedience in this sense is almost a dead letter in modern Christianity. Without doubt the popular misconception of the function of faith, and the failure of our teachers to insist upon obedience, have weakened the Church and retarded revival tragically in the last half-century. The only cure is to remove the cause. This will take some courage, but it will be worth the labor."

When Jesus gave the Great Commission, He instructed the church to make disciples in all the earth, baptize them, and "teach them to practice all the commands that I have given you" (Matt. 28:19, 20, Williams translation). We are not just to teach the believers, but are to teach them to observe, to obey, the Word of God.

The obedient life is:
I. THE PURPOSE OF OUR SALVATION

I Peter 1:2 A.N.T.: "Who were chosen and foreknown by God the Father and consecrated [sanctified, made holy] by the Spirit to be obedient to Jesus Christ, the Messiah...." It is written of Jesus Christ, that "he became the author of eternal salvation unto all them that obey him" (Heb. 5:9).

God saves us by grace, through faith (Eph. 2:8, 9) unto a life of good works and obedience (Eph. 2:10).

George B. Duncan, in a recent Keswick message, said, "You and I are elect unto obedience. This is the final fruition of God's working out of His will in our lives: that your life and mine should be a life of continual obedience to God."

II. THE PROOF OF OUR SURRENDER

John 14:15 A.N.T.: "If you really love Me you will keep [obey] My commands." Only as we are obedient to the Lord can we prove to Him that we really love Him and are really surrendered to Him (John 14:21, 23; 15:14).

III. THE PATHWAY TO OUR SUCCESS — Joshua 1:8.

Obedience to God brings: (1) success (Josh. 1:8); (2) blessings (Job 36:11; Ps. 84:11; Luke 11:28; John 13:17; James 1:25); (3) knowledge of God's will (John 7:17; Rom. 12:1, 2); (4) the reality of Christ's presence (John 14:21); (5) the presence of Christ and His Father (John 14:23); (6) abiding in His love (John 15:10); (7) answered prayer (I John 3:22).

REVIVAL BY OBEYING GOD'S WORD

All any Christian needs to do to discover the low spiritual condition into which he has drifted is to take a colored pencil and mark in the New Testament the qualities of the Christian life set forth therein. We have made tests of this with startling results.

In one church, a large city church, we challenged our hearers to make this test. A church officer who was leading the singing in the meetings did not lead the singing the next evening. One evening after the meeting I was called into the pastor's study. That church officer who abandoned his song leading was there. He said, "Pastor, since hearing this brother I have decided that I am not fit to be an officer or member of this church. I want my name taken off the church rolls. I have been a miserable hypocrite. I have been a fake Christian." Then he confessed that as a wholesale grocer he had favored a local bishop by arranging to obtain a periodic case of liquor from a liquor wholesaler for him. But after being asked to mark verses of Holy Scripture on the Christian life, he saw the verse: "Have no fellowship with the unfruitful works of darkness, but rather reprove them" (Eph. 5:11). "That verse revealed my spiritual condition, and I called up the bishop and told him I could not supply any more liquor to him, and asked him to give up his drinking. Now pastor, will you please remove my unworthy name from your membership roll?"

If we are going to have a revival in our churches, it will have to come by church people's obeying God's Word. Now obedience is just another name for revival. And we know our disobedience by what God's Word says about obedience.

— Great Commission Prayer League, Inc.

OBEDIENCE

I said, "Let me walk in the fields." He said, "No, walk in the town."
    I said, "There are no flowers there." He said, "No flowers, but a
      crown."
I said, "But the skies are black; there is nothing but noise and din."
    And He wept as He sent me back — "There is more," He said,
      "there is sin."
I cast one look at the fields, then set my face to the town;
    He said, "My child, do you yield? Will you leave the flowers for the
      crown?"
Then into His hand went mine; and into my heart came He;
    And I walk in a light divine, the path I had feared to see.

— George MacDonald

UNIT XXVIII
THE SEVEN DEMANDS OF DISCIPLESHIP

M. R. De Haan, commenting on Matthew 28:19, says: "The word 'teach' here comes from the root which means to discipline, or literally, to make disciples. Believing the preaching of the gospel makes one a believer, but those who have been made believers God now wants to go on to become disciples. The emphasis in these present days is on the making of believers, rather than on the making of real disciples. Too few are being taught to become followers of the Lord Jesus Christ, those who in addition to receiving salvation are willing to go on to follow the Lord all the way, to be taught by Him, to serve, to suffer, and if need be, to die for Him. The important thing is the desperate need of disciples today, for God uses those who know the secret of discipleship."

Here are "The Seven Demands of Discipleship" taught in the New Testament. May God help us to be "... disciples indeed" (John 8:31).

I. LOVING CHRIST MORE THAN RELATIVES.

"If any man come to me, and hate not his father, and mother, and wife, and children, and brethren, and sisters ... *he cannot be my disciple*" (Luke 14:26). The word "hate" here means "love less" and means that we should love Christ more than our relatives.

II. LOVING CHRIST MORE THAN SELF.

"If any man come to me, and hate not ... his own life also, *he cannot be my disciple*" (Luke 14:26).

III. BEARING THE CROSS.

"And whosoever doth not bear his cross, and come after me, *cannot be my disciple*" (Luke 14:27).

IV. FORSAKING ALL.

"So likewise, whosoever he be of you that forsaketh not all that he hath, *he cannot be my disciple*" (Luke 14:33).

V. CONTINUING IN HIS WORD.

"If ye continue in my word, then are ye *disciples indeed*" (John 8:31).

VI. LOVING OTHERS.

"By this shall all men know that ye are *my disciples*, if ye have love one to another" (John 13:35).

VII. BEARING MUCH FRUIT.

"Herein is my Father glorified, that ye bear much fruit; so shall ye be *my disciples*" (John 15:8).

HE LOVES JESUS MORE THAN HIS FAMILY

Hyman Appelman writes:

Some of you know that when I was converted in 1925, my people turned their faces from me. I have no standing in the family circle. When I was pastor in Vickery, Texas, my father came from Chicago to see me, to take me home. He spent eight days with me, and I came closer to hell in agony of heart and soul during those eight days than I ever expect to be in time or eternity.

I took him off the train. We hugged and kissed each other, got into my car, drove home. During those eight days, by day and by night, I tried every way, I used every way to win my father to Christ, but to no avail. He refused to even look at a New Testament. He turned His back on my Christ.

Came the day of his departure. Together we sat in the Pullman seat. Again he pled with me to turn my back on Christ and the church and my humble work, to come home. He said, "Son, Mamma's getting old, I am getting old, you are our firstborn, we have done all we could do for you, as sacrificially as we knew how. Won't you come home? We haven't much longer to live. Cheer our old age. I've got some money with me. I'll buy your ticket. Don't get off the train. We'll send for your wife. We've got plenty of money. Come home."

You turn to me, my beloved, and say, "Preacher, you love your people; why didn't you go?" I'll tell you why. All the time my daddy was weeping, all the time I was praying, all the time my heart was breaking, above his head I could see a hill, and on that hill a cross, on that cross the bleeding, broken body of my Saviour.

Beloved, I may be a Jew, but I am not a dog! If Jesus Christ loved me enough to die for me, I love Him enough, and I want you to love Him enough, so that together we may be ready to live, to give, and to go. God, give us the grace to do it for Jesus sake, Amen.

JESUS, I MY CROSS HAVE TAKEN

Jesus, I my cross have taken, all to leave and follow Thee;
Destitute, despised, forsaken, Thou, from hence, my all shalt be:
Perish every fond ambition, all I've sought, and hoped, and known;
Yet how rich is my condition, God and heaven are still my own!

— Henry F. Lyte

UNIT XXIX
SEVEN REASONS FOR REPENTANCE

Repentance is a much-neglected doctrine in the preaching of today. Some preachers and teachers say it is not necessary, that it was only for the Jews. Others seem not to know the meaning of the word and confuse people by their preaching and teaching.

The word "repentance" in the New Testament in the Greek is "metanoia," which means "to change the mind," "to have another mind," and this change of mind involves both a turning from sin and a turning to God, and it touches the intellect, emotions, and will.

Repentance was the keynote of the preaching of John the Baptist (Matt. 3:1, 2, 7, 8); of Jesus Christ (Matt. 4:17; Mark 1:14, 15; Luke 5:32); of the disciples and apostles (Mark 6:12; Acts 2:38; 3:14, 15, 19; 17:30, 31; 20:21; 26:19, 20). It is a gift of God (Acts 5:30, 31; 11:18; II Tim. 2:24, 25; II Peter 3:9); and this gift of repentance is given when people own their sin (Luke 5:21; 18:13; 23:39-43).

Here are "Seven Reasons for Repentance":

I. BECAUSE GOD'S WORD COMMANDS IT — Matthew 3:1, 2, 7, 8; 4:17; Mark 1:14, 15; 6:12; Acts 2:38; 3:14, 15, 19; 17:30, 31; 20:21; 26:19, 20.

II. BECAUSE IT IS GOD'S SUPREME DESIRE — II Peter 3:9.

III. BECAUSE OF GOD'S GOODNESS — Romans 2:4.

IV. BECAUSE THROUGH IT SINS ARE BLOTTED OUT — Acts 3:19.

V. BECAUSE THROUGH IT JOY SHALL BE IN HEAVEN — Luke 15:7, 10.

VI. BECAUSE WITHOUT IT JUDGMENT COMES — Acts 17:30, 31.

VII. BECAUSE WITHOUT IT PEOPLE PERISH — Luke 13:3, 5.

May it be true of you " . . . that the goodness of God leadeth thee to repentance" (Rom. 2:4). I pray that you will obey the command of Jesus Christ: "repent ye, and believe the gospel" (Mark 1:15).

REPENT OR PERISH

I read an interesting story recently about how God used one verse of Scripture to bring a man to repentance. William Evans, when still a student at the Moody Bible Institute, began talking to a man at the Pacific Garden Mission about his soul. The man argued, "I don't believe the Bible. I'm an atheist." Evans, knowing the Word of God never returns void, insisted on repeating one verse over and over to him: "Except ye repent, ye shall all likewise perish." The unbeliever scoffed, "I told you I don't believe the Bible." But undaunted, Evans requoted Luke 13:3. The atheist became exasperated and shouted, "You disgusting fellow, what's the use in telling me that again?" In anger he struck the young man between the eyes with his fist, but God gave the student grace to hold his temper. Getting up from the street, he retrieved his Bible and said, "My friend, God loves you, and 'except ye repent, ye shall all likewise perish.'" The man walked away in a rage. The next night, however, the atheist was at the Pacific Garden Mission long before the meeting was scheduled to open. He confessed to the superintendent, "I was not able to sleep last night; all over the walls in my room I seemed to read: 'Except ye repent, ye shall all likewise perish.' When I got up, the same words were ringing in my ears at the breakfast table, and all through the day they have troubled me. I have come back tonight to settle it all with the Lord."

I AM RESOLVED

I am resolved no longer to linger, charmed by the world's delight;
　　Things that are higher, things that are nobler, these have allured my
　　　sight.
I am resolved to go to the Saviour, leaving my sin and strife;
　　He is the true One, He is the just One, He hath the words of life.
I am resolved to follow the Saviour, faithful and true each day;
　　Heed what he sayeth, do what He willeth, He is the living way.
I am resolved to enter the kingdom, leaving the paths of sin;
　　Friends may oppose me, foes may beset me, still will I enter in.
I am resolved, and who will go with me? Come, friends, without delay,
　　Taught by the Bible, led by the Spirit, we'll walk the heavenly way.
I will hasten to Him, Hasten so glad and free,
　　Jesus, greatest, highest, I will come to Thee.

　　　　　　　　　　　　　　　— Palmer Hartsough

UNIT XXX
SEVEN REASONS WHY YOU SHOULD BE SAVED *TODAY*
II Corinthians 6:2; Hebrews 3:7, 8

I. BECAUSE YOU ARE LOST *TODAY*.

Every person who is not saved is already lost. Jesus said, "He that believeth on him [Jesus] is not condemned: but he that believeth not is condemned *already*, because he hath not believed in the name of the only begotten Son of God" (John 3:18).

II. BECAUSE YOU MAY HAVE A SERIOUS SICKNESS OR ACCIDENT *TODAY*.

God's Word warns us: "Boast not thyself of tomorrow; for thou knowest not what a day may bring forth" (Prov. 27:1).

III. BECAUSE YOU MAY DIE *TODAY*.

In the Book of Job we read, " . . . no man is sure of life" (Job 24:22), and "In a moment shall they die . . . " (Job 34:20). David said, "there is but a step between me and death" (I Sam. 20:3).

IV. BECAUSE YOU MAY GO TO HELL *TODAY*.

The Bible makes it clear that as soon as an unsaved person dies, he goes to Hell: "the rich man also died, and was buried; And in hell he lift up his eyes, being in torments . . . " (Luke 16:22, 23).

V. BECAUSE CHRIST MAY COME *TODAY*.

Jesus warned us, "Therefore be ye also ready: for in such an hour as ye think not the Son of man cometh" (Matt. 24:44). You will be left for judgment if you are not saved when He comes.

VI. BECAUSE YOU MAY CROSS GOD'S DEADLINE *TODAY*.

"He that being often reproved hardeneth his neck, shall suddenly be destroyed, and that without remedy" (Proverbs 29:1). If people continue to refuse God's call, there will come a time when He will refuse their call (see Prov. 1:24-32; John 12:35-40; Rom. 1:24, 26, 28).

VII. BECAUSE GOD WANTS YOU TO BE SAVED *TODAY*.

He invites you: "Come; for all things are *now* ready" (Luke 14:17; see also John 6:37; II Cor. 6:2; Heb. 3:7, 8). When Zacchaeus received Jesus Christ, Jesus said unto him, *"This day* is salvation come to this house . . . " (see Luke 19:1-10).

"THE HARVEST IS PASSED, THE SUMMER IS ENDED, AND I AM NOT SAVED"

In the early days of Mr. Moody's ministry in Chicago, a man who came often to the Tabernacle seemed on the verge of a decision for Christ, but because of his fear of ridicule from his business partner, he kept putting off this most important decision. One day, Moody was called to the home of this man and found him dying. As Moody approached his bed, the man said, "I don't want you to talk to me. It will do no good. I have had my chance and thrown it away." Mr. Moody quoted Scripture to him and tried to show him there was hope even in the last hour, but the man kept saying, "It is too late. I have thrown away my chance."

All that afternoon he kept repeating one passage of Scripture, "The harvest is past, the summer is ended, and I am not saved." Just as the sun was sinking, they heard him whispering in a low tone, "The harvest is past, the summer is ended, and I am not saved," and thus he went out into a Christless eternity, simply because he kept saying "Tomorrow" when God said "Today."

THE DEADLINE

There is a time, I know not when; a place, I know not where,
  Which marks the destiny of men to heaven or despair.
There is a line by us not seen, which crosses every path;
  The hidden boundary between God's patience and His wrath.
To cross that limit is to die, to die, as if by stealth.
  It may not pale the beaming eye, nor quench the glowing health.
The conscience may be still at ease, the spirit light and gay.
  That which is pleasing still may please, and care be thrust away.
But on that forehead God hath set indelibly a mark,
  By man unseen, for man as yet is blind and in the dark.
Oh, where is that mysterious bourn, by which each path is crossed,
  Beyond which God Himself hath sworn that he who goes is lost?
How long may man go on in sin, how long will God forbear?
  Where does hope end, and where begin the confines of despair?
One answer from the sky is sent, "Ye who from God depart,
  While it is called today, repent and harden not your heart."

UNIT XXXI
SEVEN STEPS TO SUCCESS IN THE CHRISTIAN LIFE

In order to be a successful Christian, you must first become a Christian. Jesus said, "Ye must be born again . . ." (John 3:7). In order to be born again, you must repent and receive Jesus Christ as personal Saviour and Lord (Acts 20:21; Luke 13:3; John 1:12, 13).

After you start right, then you need to:

I. **S**EARCH THE SCRIPTURES DAILY — Acts 17:11.

Each day you should study the Bible. The word "success" is mentioned only one time in the Bible (Josh. 1:8), and this verse tells us that we must meditate in the Bible day and night, and then obey it, in order to be a success.

II. **U**NCEASINGLY PRAY — I Thessalonians 5:17.

The Christians who amount to anything for God are like the first-century Christians who said, "But we will give ourselves continually to prayer, and to the ministry of the Word" (Acts 6:4).

III. **C**ONFESS CHRIST — Matthew 10:32, 33; Romans 10:9, 10; Acts 1:8.

Don't be ashamed of Christ — tell others about Him. "Silence is golden" is an old saying, but sometimes it's just plain "yellow."

IV. **C**ONFESS EVERY KNOWN SIN — I John 1:9.

Sin in a Christian's life will break fellowship with God, but confession will restore it. "Keep short accounts with God."

V. **E**NTER INTO THE SERVICES OF A GOOD BIBLE-PREACHING CHURCH — Hebrews 10:25.

As soon as you are saved, be baptized and enter into the fellowship and services of a good, Bible-preaching, Bible-loving, and Bible-living church (Acts 2:41, 42).

VI. **S**ET ASIDE AT LEAST ONE-TENTH OF YOUR INCOME FOR THE LORD'S WORK — I Corinthians 16:2; II Corinthians 8:7, 8; 9:6, 7.

God's people in the Old Testament were commanded to give 10 per cent to the Lord. Should we under grace in the New Testament give less?

VII. **S**URRENDER TO THE HOLY SPIRITS WORKING IN YOUR LIFE — Ephesians 5:18; Galatians 5:16.

No person can really be a success as God counts success unless he is filled with the Holy Spirit .

THE POWER OF A SUCCESSFUL CHRISTIAN LIFE

David Brainerd was a man who lived a short life, dying at the age of 29, and in his lifetime reaching very few people for Christ. Many would count him a failure. But David Brainerd's life was totally surrendered to God and for over two hundred years God has used his life to reach many other lives through Brainerd's Diary, which was read by William Carey, who was so moved by it that he went as a missionary to India. Henry Martyn read it and went as a missionary to India. Robert Murray McCheyne read it and was powerfully impressed by it. Payson read it and said he had never been so impressed by anything in his life as by the story. Oswald J. Smith read it and was so influenced by it that he named his youngest son after Brainerd, and when he was but eighteen years of age, Smith became a missionary to the Indians 3,000 miles from his home.

A. J. Gordon writes of Brainerd, "Those living such lives may soon be forgotten. The world may take no note of them. But by and by the great moving current of these lives will begin to tell as in the case of this young man not quite thirty years of age. The marvelous missionary revival of the nineteenth century is due more to his prayers than to any other thing."

Some of the statements he made in his Diary that have challenged men for over two centuries are:

"My heaven is to please God and glorify Him and to give my all to Him, and to be wholly devoted to His glory."

"There is nothing in the world worth living for but doing good and finishing God's work, doing the work that Christ did. I see nothing else in the world that can yield any satisfaction besides living to God, pleasing Him, and doing His whole will."

"There appeared to be nothing of any importance to me but holiness of heart and life, and the conversion of the heathen to God. I cared not where or how I lived, or what hardships I went through so that I could but gain souls to Christ."

THE LIFE THAT COUNTS

The life that counts must toil and fight; must hate the wrong and love
    the right;
Must stand for truth, by day, by night — this is the life that counts.
The life that counts is linked with God; and turns not from the cross —
    the rod;
But walks with joy where Jesus trod — this is the life that counts.

UNIT XXXII
SEVEN THINGS GOD SAYS WE "OUGHT" TO DO

In I Chronicles 12:32, God says that the children of Issachar "were men that had understanding of the times, to know what Israel *ought* to do. . . . " In the Bible, God tells those who are Christians what they *ought* to do. "Ought" means "owe to do."

I. WE OUGHT TO OBEY GOD — Acts 5:29.

God says, "Behold, to obey is better than sacrifice, and to hearken than the fat of rams" (I Sam. 15:22). May we say truthfully what the people said to Joshua, "The Lord our God we will serve, and his voice will we obey" (John. 24:24).

II. WE OUGHT TO HEED GOD'S WORD — Hebrews 2:1.

James 1:22 says, "But be ye doers of the word, and not hearers only, deceiving your own selves."

III. WE OUGHT TO PRAY ALWAYS — Luke 18:1.

The Pilgrim Bible has a note at this verse which reads, "On all occasions to pray or be in an attitude of prayer." I Thessalonians 5:17 says, "Pray without ceasing."

IV. WE OUGHT TO PLEASE GOD — I Thessalonians 4:1.

There are three sacrifices which are said to be well-pleasing to God: our praise (Heb. 13:15); our purse (Heb. 13:16); and our person (Romans 12:1, 2); or we could say, our songs, our substance, and our self.

V. WE OUGHT TO LOVE ONE ANOTHER — I John 4:11.

Jesus said, "By this shall all men know that ye are my disciples, if ye have love one to another" (John 13:35), and He further says in I John 3:16: "we ought to lay down our lives for the brethren."

VI. WE OUGHT TO HELP THE WEAK — Romans 15:1.

Here God is saying that those Christians who are spiritually strong "ought to bear the infirmities of the [spiritually] weak . . . " in order to help him to become a strong Christian.

VII. WE OUGHT TO WALK AS CHRIST WALKED — I John 2:6.

Jesus Christ walked, or lived, in dependence upon His Father, in obedience to Him, and in the power of the Holy Spirit, and it was said of Him that He "went about doing good . . . " (Acts 10:38). May God help us to "follow His steps" (I Peter 2:21).

EYE FOR SALE

Ted S. Rendall, Vice-President of Prairie Bible Institute, wrote this very interesting article based upon a true story related by D. R. Malsbury, missionary in South Korea, which illustrates how a Christian loved God and others:

He had two good eyes. Never had either of them given him any trouble. But he could see with one. He had tried it, and although his vision was limited to some extent, he could still get around.

Why not offer one of his good eyes to the hospital in the south? They would pay him good money, and he could — well, what could he do with the money?

He wanted to give the money to repair the church building in which he and a handful of his fellow Christians met from Sunday to Sunday. It was badly in need of some repairs. When it rained, the people inside were soaked. When it was cold, they were exposed to the bitter wind.

That's it! He would sell one of his eyes and give the money to the Lord. That would mean, of course, that he would be permanently disabled and disfigured; but he loved his Lord, and he wanted to do something for Him and for His people.

Arriving at the hospital, he offered his eye for sale; but the hospital authorities would not hear of such a thing. They immediately discouraged him and sent him back home, telling him that the members of his church should save in order to repair their church building. He should not have to sell his eye for that.

After this demonstration of love and sacrifice the members of his church did rally around, and although they were poor, desperately poor, repairs were duly made to the building.

Repairs were made, but it took one man to provide the incentive — one man with an eye for sale.

O MASTER OF THE LOVING HEART

O Master of the loving heart, the Friend of all in need,
  We pray that we may be like Thee in thought and word and deed.
Thy days were full of kindly acts; Thy speech was true and plain;
  And no one ever sought Thee, Lord, or came to Thee in vain.
O grant us hearts like Thine, dear Lord; so joyous, true and free
  That all Thy children everywhere be drawn by us to Thee.

            — Calvin W. Laufer

UNIT XXXIII
SEVEN WAYS TO KNOW IF YOU'RE GOING TO HEAVEN

Almost everyone you talk to about spiritual things plans to go to heaven some day. I have only talked to one person in my lifetime who told me he was sure he was going to hell. About 95 per cent of Americans, in a recent poll, thought there was no danger of their going to hell, and in another poll taken in America some time ago, 88 out of 100 expected to go to heaven.

Jesus said that in order for a person to go to heaven, he had to be born again (John 3:1-7). God's Word says that there are tests, or ways, by which we may know whether we have been born again. There are at least seven of them given in I John. In this short book of five chapters, the phrases "born of God," or "born of him," are used seven times: 2:29; 3:9 (twice); 4:7; 5:1, 4, 18; and the word "know" is used 27 times; "knoweth," 6 times; "known," 5 times; and "knew," once, making it clear and plain that we can know that we have been born again and are going to heaven. May you "Examine yourselves, whether you are in the faith . . ." (II Cor. 13:5).

I. IF YOU ARE GOING TO HEAVEN, YOU WILL OBEY GOD'S WORD — I John 2:3-5; Matthew 7:21-23; John 8:47; Hebrews 5:9.

II. IF YOU ARE GOING TO HEAVEN, YOU WILL PRACTICE RIGHTEOUSNESS — I John 2:29.

III. IF YOU ARE GOING TO HEAVEN, YOU WILL NOT PRACTICE SIN — I John 3:9.

"No one born (begotten) of God [deliberately and knowingly] habitually practices sin, for God's nature abides in him . . ." (A.N.T.).

IV. IF YOU ARE GOING TO HEAVEN, YOU HAVE THE WITNESS OF THE HOLY SPIRIT — I John 3:24; 4:13; 5:10; Romans 8:16.

V. IF YOU ARE GOING TO HEAVEN, YOU WILL LOVE OTHER CHRISTIANS — I John 3:14; 4:7.

VI. IF YOU ARE GOING TO HEAVEN, YOU BELIEVE THAT JESUS IS THE CHRIST — I John 5:1, 13.

VII. IF YOU ARE GOING TO HEAVEN, YOU OVERCOME THE WORLD — I John 5:4, 5.

If you have examined yourself and found that you have never been born again, receive Jesus Christ as your personal Saviour and Lord right now and God will make you His child, and you will then be "born of God" and know you are going to Heaven (John 1:12, 13).

HE KNOWS NOW THAT HE IS GOING TO HEAVEN

My friend, Pastor Howard "Barney" Barnes, tells how he tried for seventeen years to get to heaven:

Are you trying to get ready for heaven? Before I gave it up as a bad job I tried for seventeen years. It all started when I was thirteen.

Our Sunday School teacher requested his class of problem boys to attend revival services. In response to an invitation I went forward and knelt in prayer. I was going to "get ready for heaven." While attempting to pray the only prayer I knew (the Lord's Prayer), I was constantly interrupted by expressions of encouragement from well-meaning church-members. They alternately advised me to "hold on," "let go," and "pray through." At last one of the leaders bent down and spoke in my ear, "Are you all right?" Thinking he was concerned about my physical welfare, I answered in the affirmative. He stood me on my feet and shouted, "Praise the Lord, he's saved!" If I was saved I did not know it.

While still in my teens I attended revival services at another church. At the insistence of an elderly lady I knelt at an altar. Again I was going to "get ready for heaven." She pointed to a decorative cross on the wall and asked, "Can't you see Jesus dying on the cross?" Closing my eyes and recalling pictures of the crucifixion I answered, "Yes." The dear lady was overjoyed as she shouted aloud the news, "This boy is saved!" Actually I was only confused.

At the age of 26 I married and settled down to a normal American life. Some three years after our marriage my wife and I attended a nearby Bible-preaching church. My wife dedicated her life to the Lord. I renewed my efforts to "get ready for heaven."

One night in January, 1950, I knelt in my living room, confessed my self to be a poor lost sinner, and trusted in the finished work of Christ as my only hope. From John 6:37 I learned that Jesus would not reject those who truly came to Him. Because I *knew* I had come to Him, the *assurance* of that promise satisfied the longings of my heart. After seventeen years I quit "trying" and started "trusting."

WE CAN KNOW

Why do folks struggle through this life and never seem to know
That when they leave this "vale of tears" to Heaven they will go?
Must we exist with fear and doubts, uncertainty and strife?
Or can we know the peace of God, possess eternal life?
Many Scriptures reveal it clear and positive, indeed,
That we can have a "know-so" faith — assurance for our need!

— Roy J. Wilkins

UNIT XXXIV
SEVEN WAYS TO LIMIT GOD
Psalm 78:41

L. L. Legters, in his book, *God's Fellow-Workers*, says, "There are many things that baffle human understanding, but one of the most perplexing questions is, Why God should have limited Himself to human beings in His work of seeking sons and saving men? We remember that God used only the Spirit of God, the Word of God, and redeemed lives. It is easy to understand His working through the Holy Spirit, who is faithful, and through the Word, which never changes, but why He should have limited Himself to men, even though they are redeemed, is beyond understanding.

"God is limited by His fellow-workers both in the blessings which He would give to them individually and to others through them."

In Psalm 78, God speaks of the ways His people limited Him in that day. Just as they limited God, so can we today. Here are some of the ways to limit God:

I. LIMITING GOD BY BACKSLIDING.
". . . Israel . . . turned back in the day of battle" (Ps. 78:9)

II. LIMITING GOD BY DISOBEDIENCE.
"They kept not the covenant of God, and refused to walk in his law" (Ps. 78:10).

III. LIMITING GOD BY FORGETFULNESS.
"And forgot his works, and his wonders that he had shewed them" (Ps. 78:11, 42).

IV. LIMITING GOD BY MURMURING.
"Yea, they spake against God . . ." (Ps. 78:19).

V. LIMITING GOD BY UNBELIEF.
"Because they believed not in God, and trusted not in his salvation" (Ps. 78:22, 32).

VI. LIMITING GOD BY INSINCERITY.
"Nevertheless they did flatter him with their mouth, and they lied unto him with their tongues. For their heart was not right with him, neither were they steadfast in his covenant" (Ps. 78:36, 37).

VII. LIMITING GOD BY UNFAITHFULNESS.
"But turned back, and dealt unfaithfully like their fathers . . ." (Ps. 78:57).

"I CANNOT USE YOU NOW"

F. B. Meyer, speaking at Keswick, used this illustration which shows how our sins limit God as to what He will do for us and through us. He took from his pocket a fountain pen and said, "This is my pen; I have had it for years. It wrote all my letters, it signed my name again and again. This is my pen, but I do not use it now, I use this one." Then he took another pen from his pocket, and said, "I sometimes imagine that first pen says to me, 'Master, why don't you use me? You used me all those years. I wrote your letters, I signed your checks, and I was always in your hand, always being used by you; why don't you use me now?' And I said to my pen, 'Pen, you are still mine, and you are in my pocket, and near to my heart; you are dear to me because I bought you, but I cannot use you now because every time I use you you defile my hands; you are not clean.'"

IS THIS CONSECRATION?

I'll go where you want me to go, dear Lord.
  Real service is what I desire;
I'll say what you want me to say, dear Lord —
  But don't ask me to sing in the choir.

I'll say what you want me to say, dear Lord,
  I like to see things come to pass;
But don't ask me to teach girls and boys, dear Lord —
  I'd rather just stay in my class.

I'll do what you want me to do, dear Lord,
  I yearn for the kingdom to thrive;
I'll give you my nickels and dimes, dear Lord —
  But please don't ask me to tithe.

I'll go where you want me to go, dear Lord,
  I'll say what you want me to say;
I'm busy just now with myself, dear Lord —
  I'll help you some other day.

UNIT XXXV
"SURE SITTING PRETTY, AREN'T WE?"

Donald G. Barnhouse related this story in one of his messages:

Once I was preaching in my church on what God says He has done with our sins. I noticed a boy about fourteen years of age sitting in the gallery. He had his hands and his chin on the railing, and had pulled himself forward on the seat, and the intensity with which he was listening made an impression on me. When I finished preaching I went to the back of the church and was greeting people as they went out, and I saw this lad. He walked as a schoolboy will, and when I had finished talking to someone all of a sudden he pulled my jacket, and said, "Good sermon, Doc." Then as I looked at him he said, "Sure sitting pretty, aren't we?"

Yes, those of us who have repented of our sins and received Jesus Christ as our Saviour and Lord are surely "sitting pretty." Here is what the Bible says God has done with the sins of the saved.

I. OUR SINS ARE FORGIVEN — I John 2:12.

II. OUR SINS ARE FORGOTTEN — Hebrews 8:12.

III. OUR SINS ARE CLEANSED — I John 1:7.

IV. OUR SINS ARE GONE — Hebrews 9:26.

V. OUR SINS ARE ATONED FOR — Isaiah 53:5, 6.

VI. OUR SINS ARE COVERED — Psalm 32:1.

VII. OUR SINS ARE BLOTTED OUT — Isaiah 44:22.

VIII. OUR SINS ARE REMOVED — Psalm 103:12.

IX. OUR SINS ARE CAST BEHIND GOD'S BACK — Isaiah 38:17.

X. OUR SINS ARE NO MORE REMEMBERED — Hebrews 10:17.

XI. OUR SINS ARE SUBDUED — Micah 7:19.

XII. OUR SINS ARE NOT IMPUTED TO US — Romans 4:8.

XIII. OUR SINS ARE PARDONED — Micah 7:18.

XIV. OUR SINS ARE MADE WHITE AS SNOW — Isaiah 1:18.

XV. OUR SINS ARE PURGED — Hebrews 1:3.

XVI. OUR SINS ARE WASHED — Revelation 1:5.

XVII. OUR SINS ARE REMITTED — Acts 10:43.

XVIII. OUR SINS ARE NAILED TO THE CROSS — Colossians 2:14.

XIX. OUR SINS ARE TAKEN AWAY — I John 3:5.

"I WANT TO BE SAVED NOW"

Henry Moorhouse, during his first visit to America in evangelistic work, was the guest of a cultured and wealthy gentleman who had a daughter just coming into womanhood. One day she entered the library and found him reading his Bible. Looking up, calling her by name, he said in his quiet kindly way, "Are you saved?"

She could only reply, "No, Mr. Moorhouse, I am not." Then came another question, "Would you like to be saved?" She thought for a moment of all that is meant by salvation, and of all that is meant by the lack of salvation, and she frankly answered, "Yes, I wish I were a sincere Christian." Then came the tender appeal, "Would you like to be saved now?" She replied, "Yes, I want to be saved now."

The supreme moment in her life was reached. Mr. Moorhouse asked her to kneel beside him and to read aloud the fifty-third chapter of Isaiah. This she did in a tone that became tremulous and broken by sobs. "Read it again," said Mr. Moorhouse gently, "and where you find 'we,' 'our,' and 'us,' put in 'I,' 'my,' and 'me.'"

The weeping girl read it again. "He is despised and rejected of men; a man of sorrows, and acquainted with grief; and I hid as it were my face from him; he was despised, and I esteemed him not. Surely he hath borne my griefs, and carried my sorrows; yet I did esteem Him stricken, smitten of God, and afflicted. He was wounded for my transgressions, he was bruised for my iniquities: the chastisement of my peace was upon him; and with his stripes I am healed."

With deep emotion she asked, "Oh, Mr. Moorhouse, is this true?" "Dear child," he answered, "does not God say it?"

She was silent for a time, but at length looking up, no longer through the tears of sorrow, but in joy and adoring gratitude and in-expressible love, she said, "Then I am saved, for all my iniquities have been laid upon Him, and no stroke remains for me." She arose from her knees with the peace of God filling her heart and soul.

NOTHING TO PAY

Nothing to pay! the debt is so great. What will you do with the awful
    weight?
  Hear the voice of Jesus say; "Verily thou hast nothing to pay.
All has been put to My account, I have paid the full amount."
  Blotted it out with His bleeding hand! Free and forgiven, and loved,
    you stand.
Hear the voice of Jesus say, "Verily thou hast nothing to pay!
  Paid is the debt, and the debtor free! Now I ask thee, lovest thou
    Me?"

UNIT XXXVI
"TAKE HEED"

These two words are used over sixty times in the Bible. Paul used them nine times and Jesus used them sixteen times. They have the meaning of "be careful," "beware," "be on your guard," "take care."

I. TAKE HEED HOW YOU BUILD — "But let every man *take heed* how he buildeth thereupon" (I Cor. 3:10).

Here Paul tells us who are Christians to be careful and be on our guard as to how we live our Christian lives, since one day at the Judgment Seat of Christ, our works that we have built upon the foundation, Jesus Christ (I Cor. 3:11), will be tested and tried, and some shall suffer loss if their works did not glorify God (I Cor. 3:9-15; II Cor. 5:10, 11).

II. TAKE HEED LEST YOU FALL — "Wherefore let him that thinketh he standeth *take heed* lest he fall" (I Cor. 10:12).

God's Word tells us how to keep from falling in II Peter 1:5-10, and promises us "if ye do these things [the things mentioned in verses 5-8] ye shall never fall" (v. 10).

III. TAKE HEED CONCERNING AN EVIL HEART OF UNBELIEF — "*Take heed,* brethren, lest there be in any of you an evil heart of unbelief, in departing from the living God" (Heb. 3:12). "Believe in the Lord your God, so shall ye be established: believe his prophets, so shall ye prosper" (II Chron. 20:20).

IV. TAKE HEED WHAT YOU HEAR — Jesus said, "*Take heed* what ye hear . . . " (Mark 4:24).

"So then faith cometh by hearing, and hearing by the Word of God" (Rom. 10:17), so we should be careful as to what we listen to, since Jesus has warned us: "And many false prophets shall rise, and shall deceive many" (Matt. 24:11).

V. TAKE HEED HOW YOU HEAR — "*Take heed* therefore how ye hear . . . " (Luke 8:18).

In the parable preceding this verse (Luke 8:5-15), Jesus spoke of four different kinds of hearers, and He wants us to be a "good ground" hearer who hears the Word, obeys it, and brings forth fruit (v. 15).

VI. TAKE HEED THAT YOU BE NOT DECEIVED — "And he said, *Take heed* that ye be not deceived . . . " (Luke 21:8).

VII. TAKE HEED THAT YOU BE READY FOR CHRIST'S COMING — "And take heed to yourselves, lest . . . that day come upon you unawares" (Luke 21:34-36).

Make sure that you are ready by repenting of your sins and receiving Jesus Christ as your personal Saviour and Lord (Luke 13:3).

TAKE HEED HOW YOU BUILD

M. R. De Haan shares this story of a careless builder:

A wealthy man before embarking on an extended tour of Europe, said to his contractor, "While I am away, I want you to build me a fine home according to these plans. Be sure you work with extreme care, and use the best of everything. Tell me the cost as soon as you have it and I'll give you my check." During the process of construction the contractor discovered many opportunities for substituting inferior materials and pocketing the money thus saved. His employer would never know the difference, and he himself would profit thereby. But he soon regretted his dishonesty, for the wealthy man upon his return inspected the finished home and said: "You have built it exactly as I wanted it, and I'm sure that you used the best of everything in its construction. Now, in appreciation of your long years of service to me, I am giving you this new home for your very own. Here's the deed!" Friend, your house of life is like that: you choose the materials that go into it, and you may substitute inferior quality at places where you think it will not be seen; but if anything goes wrong with the deal, you will be the one who suffers most. We are building for eternity! The house we will have later will depend on the material we use now.

HIS PLAN FOR ME . . .

When I stand at the judgment seat of Christ, and He shows me His
    plan for me,
  The plan of my life as it might have been had He had His way, and
    I see
How I blocked Him here, and I checked Him there, and I would not
    yield my will —
  Will there be grief in my Saviour's eyes, grief, though He loves me
    still?
He would have me rich, and I stand there poor, stripped of all but
    His grace,
  While memory runs like a hunted thing down the paths I cannot
    retrace.
Then my desolate heart will well-nigh break with the tears that I
    cannot shed;
  I shall cover my face with my empty hands, I shall bow my un-
    crowned head.
Lord, of the years that are left to me, I give them to Thy hand;
  Take me, and break me, and mold me to the pattern Thou hast
    planned.

— Martha Snell Nicholson

UNIT XXXVII
THIRTY-THIRD DEGREE CHRISTIANS

At the very instant a person receives Christ, he is brought by God into at least thirty-three distinct positions.

I. He Forgave Us (Eph. 1:7; Acts 10:43).

II. He Regenerated Us (John 3:3-7; 1:12, 13).

III. He Made Us Alive (John 5:25; Eph. 2:1).

IV. He Justified Us (Rom. 5:1; Acts 13:38, 39).

V. He Adopted and Made Us Children of God (Eph. 1:5; John 1:12).

VI. He Perfected Us Forever (Heb. 10:14).

VII. He Cleansed and Washed Us (Rev. 1:5; Titus 3:5).

VIII. He Baptized Us by the Spirit into One Body (I Cor. 12:13).

IX. He Sealed Us by the Spirit (Eph. 1:13; 4:30).

X. He Made Us the Temple of the Holy Spirit (I Cor. 6:19).

XI. He Brought Us into Vital Union with Christ (John 15:1-7).

XII. He Delivered Us and Translated Us into the Kingdom of His Dear Son (Col. 1:13).

XIII. He Raised Us and Made Us to Sit Together with Christ in the Heavenlies (Eph. 2:6).

XIV. He Opened Our Eyes Spiritually (Acts 26:18).

XV. He Turned Us from Darkness to Light (John 8:12; Acts 26:18).

XVI. He Gave Us Rest (Matt. 11:28:29).

XVII. He Gave Us Eternal Life (John 3:16; 5:24; 10:28).

XVIII. He Made Us Saints (Rom. 1:7; I Cor. 1:2).

XIX. He Sanctified Us (Heb. 10:14).

XX. He Delivered Us from Condemnation (John 5:24; Rom. 8:1).

XXI. He Made Us Free (John 8:36; Rom. 8:2).

XXII. He Gave Us Peace (Rom. 5:1; Eph. 2:14, 17; John 14:27).

XXIII. He Took Us into His Hands for Safekeeping (John 10:28-30).

XXIV. He Made Us a New Creation (II Cor. 5:17).

XXV. He Delivered Us from This Present Evil Age (Gal. 1:4).

XXVI. He Made Us His Heritage (Eph. 1:11, 18).

XXVII. He Made Us Complete in Christ (Col. 2:10).

XXVIII. He Gave Us Access into His Grace (Rom. 5:2).

XXIX. He Delivered Us from the Curse of the Law (Gal. 3:13).

XXX. He Made Us Abraham's Spiritual Seed (Gal. 3:29; Rom. 4:16).

XXXI. He Made Us Heirs of God and Joint Heirs with Christ (Gal. 3:29; 4:7; Rom. 8:16, 17).

XXXII. He Made Us a Royal Priesthood, a Holy Nation, a Peculiar People (I Peter 2:9).

XXXIII. He Blessed Us with All Spiritual Blessings in the Heavenlies in Christ (Eph. 1:3).

"BLANKETS OR NO BLANKETS, HALLELUJAH!"

A good Presbyterian minister in old Scotland, of the staid and orthodox type, had in his congregation a poor old woman who was in the habit of saying, "Praise the Lord!" "Amen!" when anything particularly helpful was said.

This practice greatly disturbed the minister, and one New Year's day he went to see her. "Betty," he said, "I'll make a bargain with you. You call out 'Praise the Lord' just when I get to the best part of my sermon, and it upsets my thoughts. Now if you will stop doing it all this year, I'll give you a pair of wool blankets." Betty was poor, and the offer of the blankets looked very good. So she did her best to earn them.

Sunday after Sunday she kept quiet. But one day a minister of another type came to preach — a man bubbling over with joy. As he preached on *the forgiveness of sins and of all the blessings that follow*, the vision of the blankets began to fade and fade, and the joys of salvation grew brighter and brighter. At last Betty could stand it no longer, and jumping up she cried, "Blankets or no blankets, *Hallelujah!*"

WHEN ALL THY MERCIES, O MY GOD

When all Thy mercies, O my God,
  My rising soul surveys,
Transported with the view,
  I'm lost in wonder, love, and praise.
Unnumbered comforts to my soul,
  Thy tender care bestowed,
Before my infant heart conceived
  From whom those comforts flowed.
Ten thousand thousand precious gifts
  My daily thanks employ;
Nor is the least a cheerful heart
  That tastes those gifts with joy.
Through all eternity to Thee
  A grateful song I'll raise;
But oh, eternity's too short
  To utter all Thy praise!
               — Joseph Addison

UNIT XXXVIII
THREE NEW THINGS FOR THE NEW YEAR
Joshua 3:1-5

As we approach the New Year, our thoughts turn to new experiences. As I read the passage of Scripture above, I saw three new things for the New Year.

I. NEW WAY.

"... that ye may know the *way* by which ye must go: for ye have not passed this *way* heretofore" (v. 4). Yes, the way we go this year will be a new way — "ye have not passed this way heretofore" —but thanks be to God, "... he knoweth the *way* that I take..." (Job 23:10), and He promises us "that ye may know the *way* which ye must go..." (Josh. 3:4).

We have His promise: "I will instruct thee and teach thee in the *way* which thou shalt go: I will guide thee with mine eye" (Ps. 32:8). "Many things about tomorrow I don't seem to understand;

But I know Who holds tomorrow, and I know Who holds my hand."
— Ira Stanphill

II. NEW WALK.

"Sanctify yourselves..." (v. 5a). For this New Way for the New Year, God wants us to have a New Walk. When God said, "Sanctify yourselves," He was referring both to ceremonial and external cleansing, and moral and internal cleansing. He wants His people to be cleansed from all sin (II Cor. 7:1; II Tim. 2:21; I John 1:7; 3:2, 3).

Arthur Pink comments: "It was a call for them to cleanse themselves and dedicate themselves unto the Lord their God."

III. NEW WONDERS.

"... for tomorrow the Lord will do *wonders* among you" (v. 5b). God is the God of wonders: "Thou are the God that doest *wonders* ..." (Ps. 77:14). If we would "sanctify" ourselves in the sense of cleansing ourselves and dedicating ourselves wholly to the Lord, He would do wonders among us this year. He has promised "... to show himself strong in the behalf of them whose heart is perfect toward Him" (II Chron. 16:9).

May this New Year for us be a "New Walk" for this "New Way" so that we may see "New Wonders."

A NEW WALK BRINGS NEW WONDERS

Lee Roberson relates this story of God's wonders in a church when the people "sanctified themselves" and got right with God and each other:

Some years ago I conducted a revival in a southern town. The first four or five nights very little happened. The crowds were small. Interest was light. I detected that something was wrong in the church. There were some men who were not right in their attitude toward the pastor. They had been fighting his ministry. They had tried to defeat him in his work of soul-winning. It was also evident that the pastor's heart had been somewhat affected by this wrong relationship. One day, more or less by accident, I saw one of the four men involved in the difficulty. The pastor's remarks about him were not too kind, and I detected that here was the reason for the slowness of the revival.

And then there came a service; when I gave a message, much as I am speaking this morning, then God began working. When the invitation was given, the four men walked down the aisle. All of them were in tears. They knelt at the front of the church and in a moment, when I saw what was happening, I told the pastor I thought it would be a fine thing if he would kneel with them. He did so and in a few moments they were all standing on their feet with their arms around one another. They had confessed their sins unto the Lord and things had been made right. They had also confessed their difficulties one to another.

Did revival come? Suffice it to say that over 240 people were converted in less than a week's time, in a single church meeting. Most of them were received into the church and were baptized before the closing of the meeting. The revival was so sweeping that crowds came until the police had to close the doors to keep people out.

THE NEW YEAR'S THREE-POINT MESSAGE TO ME

I asked the Lord for some motto sweet, some rule of life with which
    to guide my feet;
    I asked, and paused; He answered soft and low: "God's will to
    know."
"Will knowledge then suffice, dear Lord?" I cried; and ere the question into silence died,
    The answer came: "Nay, but remember, too, God's will to do."
Once more I asked, "Is there no more to tell?" and once more the answer sweetly fell:
    "Yes! this one thing, all other things above, God's will to love."

UNIT XXXIX
THREE THINGS I WANT FOR CHRISTMAS

"What do you want for Christmas?"

This question is asked many times by friends and loved ones as Christmas approaches. Here are three things I want for Christmas.

I. THE REVIVAL OF THE SAINTS.

As I travel in evangelistic work from church to church and state to state, I find that one of the greatest needs in our churches is the need for revival among the people of God. Charles G. Finney gave this definition of revival: "A revival is the renewal of the first love of Christians, resulting in the awakening and conversion of sinners to God. It consists in the return of a church from her backslidings, and in the conversion of sinners." My prayer to God is, "Wilt thou not revive us again: that thy people may rejoice in thee?" (Ps. 85:6).

II. THE REGENERATION OF THE SINNERS.

I long for sinners to be saved. I pray for sinners to be saved. I know that if people are not saved they are on their way to an eternal hell, to be forever separated from God. I travel over this country preaching the Word of God, warning people to "flee from the wrath to come" (Matt. 3:7); beseeching them to be "reconciled to God (II Cor. 5:20); reminding them of Jesus' command, "Ye must be born again" (John 3:7); pleading with them to receive Jesus Christ as their personal Saviour so that they will be born again (John 1:12, 13). "Brethren, my heart's desire and prayer to God for [people] is, that they may be saved" (Rom. 10:1).

III. THE RETURN OF THE SAVIOUR.

As I see sin on every hand, as I see the awful condition this country and the world is in, and realize that things and people are going to get even worse (II Tim. 3:13), my heart cries out the last prayer of the Bible, "Even so, come, Lord Jesus" (Rev. 22:20). Christ wants us to "love his appearing," and offers "a crown of righteousness . . ." to all who do (II Tim. 4:8). In the meantime, I want to obey His command, "Occupy till I come" (Luke 19:13).

The time is short! If thou wouldst work for God it must be now;
If thou wouldst win the garland for thy brow, redeem the time.
With His reward He comes; He tarries not; His day is near;
When men least look for Him will He be here; prepare for Him!

— H. Bonar

THE BLESSINGS OF REVIVAL

I have just read, with great blessing, of a revival in a Baptist church in Auburn, New York. R. S. Stanfield writes about it:

How would you like to experience revival? Second Baptist Church in Auburn, New York, had the joy of such an experience which began on November 11, 1951. It lasted for two months.

After the revival started meetings were held in the church auditorium each evening for the next six weeks; in other words, regular services were held for forty-two consecutive evenings, and all other church activities were suspended. Three evening meetings were held during each of the seventh and eighth weeks. These meetings were largely informal, yet orderly. They were introduced generally by a verse or two of a hymn, followed by a short Scripture passage and then a few comments on the Scripture. Then the meeting was opened for testimonies, and closed with all on their knees praying. For the first two weeks the testimonies were mostly confined to personal, public confession of sins, largely the sin of criticism. During the remainder of the revival the testimonies mainly struck a note of joy and victory. Many became burdened for their loved ones and friends.

Scores of cold church members were revived, many lost souls were saved, backsliders were restored to strong faith, the timid were given boldness to witness for Christ, several broken families were reunited, organizations resolved their differences and learned to live together in a spirit of love and harmony, young people yielded their lives to the Lord, wounds of long standing were healed, restitution was made where possible, many people publicly and privately confessed their sins and forgave one another and a tragic and ever-widening church schism of six years' duration involving about one hundred adults that had left the church was gloriously healed. This schism had divided families, separated life-long friends, broken homes and undermined evangelical work throughout a broad area. These and many other blessings came as the result of the sudden visitation of the Holy Spirit in power. A spirit of unity and forgiveness prevailed such as the church had never known before in its history.

BLESSED HOPE

This is the hope that sustains us, this is our lamp in the night,
   This is the beacon we follow, waiting till faith becomes sight.
This is our heart's choicest treasures, balm for our sorrow and pain,
   Words that are precious as rubies, "Christ Jesus is coming again!"
                                        — Martha Snell Nicholson

UNIT XL
THREE QUESTIONS ABOUT SALVATION

Salvation is a great word, and is used many times in the Bible. Let us ask and answer three questions about salvation.

I. "ARE THERE FEW THAT BE SAVED?"

This was asked Jesus as He was going toward Jerusalem (Luke 13:23). In answer to this question, Jesus said, "Strive to enter in at the strait gate: for many, I say unto you, will seek to enter in, and shall not be able" (Luke 13:24). He said also, in Matthew 7:14: "Because strait is the gate, and narrow is the way, which leadeth unto life, and few there be that find it."

Carl M. Sweazy says in his book, *Evangelism That Evangelizes,* "Conservatively speaking, four-fifths of the human race are on their way to the 'lake of fire' and billions of persons of this generation, your generation and mine, are eternally doomed." Oswald Chambers, in his book, *My Utmost for His Highest,* made the statement that it was his conviction that only 15 per cent of all professing Christians had actually been saved. R. A. Torrey said he believed that only 10 per cent of those who profess to be saved were really converted. Robert G. Lee, former president of the Southern Baptist Convention, estimates that only one out of ten members in Southern Baptist Churches is saved. Franklin Logsdon estimates that only 2 per cent of the population of the world are saved, 98 per cent are lost. It is sad, but true, that there are few saved, comparatively speaking.

II. "WHO THEN CAN BE SAVED?"

Jesus' disciples asked this question in Matthew 19:25. The Bible answers this question clearly: *all can be saved* — "Who [God] will have *all men to be saved* ..." (I Tim. 2:4); "The Lord ... is long-suffering to usward, not willing that any should perish, but that *all should come to repentance*" (II Peter 3:9). (See also Isa. 45:22; Ezek. 33:11; Matt. 22:9; Luke 19:10; John 3:16; 6:37; Rom. 11:32; Rev. 22:17.) Jesus gave the reason why all will not be saved in John 5:40: "And ye will not come to me, that ye might have life."

III. "WHAT MUST I DO TO BE SAVED?"

The Philippian jailer asked this question (Acts 16:30), and it is answered in the next verse: "Believe on the Lord Jesus Christ, and thou shalt be saved ..." (Acts 16:31). A person must repent and receive Christ as personal Saviour and Lord to be saved (Acts 20:21; Rom. 10:9, 10, 13; Eph. 2:8, 9).

Are you in the "few" who are saved, or in the "many" that are lost? (Matt. 7:13, 14).

HOW THE JAILER AT PHILIPPI WAS CAUGHT

Henry Bosch relates this interesting story about Valentine Burke:

While holding a series of evangelistic meetings in St. Louis, D. L. Moody preached on the text in Acts 16:31. The following day the *Globe Democrat* reported the sermon under the sensational headline: "How the Jailer at Philippi Was Caught." A copy of the newspaper found its way into the city prison and ultimately fell into the hands of one of the most notorious criminals of that day, Valentine Burke. Having already spent half of his life behind bars, he was then awaiting trial on a fresh charge. Glancing at the headlines he thought it was jail news and began to read, rubbing his hands in glee thinking the jailer had been caught in his own trap. He once had passed through a little town in Illinois called Philippi and he decided that this must be the place to which the article referred. However, he found the story quite strange for he constantly ran across the words, "Believe on the Lord Jesus Christ and thou shalt be saved." In disgust he threw the paper away muttering about that "religious stuff." However, the words refused to leave his mind. His whole guilty past came up before him and he began to think of the coming judgment. Like the jailer of Paul's day, Burke — in his cell at midnight — finally cried to God for mercy and forgiveness. Believing on Christ he found great joy and soon fell into a peaceful sleep. The next morning for the first time the officer found the hardened sinner completely subdued and meek.

Burke served a reduced sentence, and, due to his Christian conduct, was later offered a position as deputy by the sheriff who had apprehended him. As long as he lived, Valentine Burke remained at the St. Louis prison — faithful to his Lord, and a shining witness to other needy sinners.

SALVATION IS FREE

Are you lost, my friend, do you wander alone?
Are you sick and discouraged with this world as your home?
Have you found the world empty, and futile its goal?
Do you stand alone friendless, with no joy in your soul?
Ah, friend, there's a fountain supplied by His grace,
That will wash away burdens and bring peace in their place!
There's a Saviour who's waiting His glory to share;
He paid the full price, all your sins He did bear.
Won't you come, friend, right now, won't you answer His plea?
It's the gift of redemption, yes, salvation is free!

— Florence Pauline Houk

UNIT XLI
TURN OR BURN
Ezekiel 33:11

That great evangelist of years ago, Richard Baxter, used to say over and over to his congregations, "Turn or burn." God's Word makes it plain that if people do not *turn* from their sins and receive Christ as their personal Saviour and Lord, they will *burn* forever in hell. Psalm 7:11-13 says: "God judgeth the righteous, and God is angry with the wicked every day. If he [the sinner] turn not, he [God] will whet his sword; he hath bent his bow, and made it ready. He hath also prepared for him the instruments of death...." Let me share with you four things which God says to me in our text.

I. GOD HAS NO PLEASURE IN THE DEATH OR DAMNATION OF THE SINNER.

Ezekiel 33:11a — "I have no pleasure in the death of the wicked. ..." (II Peter 3:9).

A. He has given us the Bible (II Tim. 3:16; John 20:31).

B. He has sent His Son to die for us (John 3:16, 17; Romans 5:8).

C. He has sent His Holy Spirit to speak to us (Rev. 22:17; John 16:7-9).

D. He has sent His messengers to speak to us (I Cor. 1:21; Rom. 10:21; II Chron. 36:15, 16).

E. He has been patient with us and kept us alive these many years (II Peter 3:9; Rom. 15:5).

II. GOD HAS COMMANDED US TO TURN FROM OUR WAY.

Ezekiel 33:11b — "the wicked turn from his way...."
(Acts 17:30; 20:21; 26:19, 20; II Peter 3:9; Isa. 55:7; Luke 13:3, 5).

"Repentance is not only desirable, but it is imperative and all important. Apart from it no sinner will ever be saved" — H. A. Ironside.

III. IF WE TURN WE SHALL LIVE FOREVER.

Ezekiel 33:11c — "and live...."

(I Thess. 1:9, 10; John 3:16, 36; John 5:24; 10:27-29; Romans 6:23; I John 5:11-13).

IV. IF WE DON'T TURN WE SHALL BURN FOREVER.

Ezekiel 33:11d — "why will ye die?"
(Psalm 7:12, 13; 9:17; Matt. 10:28; 25:41, 46; Mark 9:43-48; Luke 13:3; John 3:16; Rev. 14:11; Rev. 20:14, 15; Jude 13).

"GET ME OUT OF THIS PLACE — IT'S ON FIRE"

Some years ago when I was a pastor, there lived in the community where my church was located, a young man whose name was James. He never came to church but was often seen with the wrong crowd, and frequently was intoxicated. One night, in his drunken condition, he sat on the railroad track and an engine hit him, threw him aside, and he was seriously injured. He was rushed to a nearby hospital, where I was called shortly afterward to see him. The doctors thought he would not live through the night. I pleaded with James to put his trust in Jesus Christ before it was too late. He finally promised me, "Preacher, not tonight, but before I leave this hospital I will become a Christian." I prayed with him and left him, never expecting to see him alive again. But James did live and I visited him a number of times in the hospital, talking with him about being saved, and leaving tracts for him to read.

Finally, James was sent home in a cast to recuperate. When I visited him in his home I asked him, "James, did you keep your promise and become a Christian before you left the hospital?" James ashamedly admitted, "No, I didn't. But I am interested."

James became impatient with his cast, so one day he took a knife and cut it, stepped out of it, walked out of his house, and joined his friends downtown. He began his drinking again and had to be carried home drunk. He was then rushed back to the hospital and before I knew he was there, I received a telephone call, "Did you hear what happened to James?" "No, what happened?" "He had to be rushed to the hospital again." Before I could visit him, I received another call, "Did you hear what happened to James? He just died. And did you hear how he died? They had to strap him to his bed and he died crying out, 'Get me out of this place — it's on fire. Get me out of this place — it's on fire.'"

I preached James' funeral with a heavy heart, fully realizing that because he didn't *turn* to Christ, he would have to *burn* in hell. May God help you to turn to Christ now.

WHY *WILL* YE DIE?

Sinners, turn; why will ye die? God, your Maker, asks you why:
  God, Who did your being give, made you with Himself to live.
Will ye not His grace receive? Will ye still refuse to live?
  Why, ye long-sought sinners, why will ye grieve your God, and die?

UNIT XLII
TWENTY THINGS THE LORD'S SECOND COMING SHOULD CAUSE US TO BE
I John 3:2, 3

The second coming of Christ is one of the most practical doctrines in the Bible. Christ's second coming is mentioned 318 times in the New Testament, one verse in every twenty-five.

The truth that He could come at any moment should cause us:

I. TO BE FAITHFUL — Matthew 25:19-30; Luke 12:42-48; 19:12-27.

II. TO BE READY — Matthew 24:44; 25:13.

III. TO BE PURE — I John 3:2, 3.

IV. TO BE PATIENT — I Thessalonians 1:4-10; Hebrews 10:32-37; James 5:1-8; I Peter 1:7; 4:13.

V. TO BE SOBER — I Thessalonians 5:2-6; I Peter 1:13; 4:7.

VI. TO BE OBEDIENT — I Timothy 6:13, 14.

VII. TO BE SINCERE AND WITHOUT OFFENSE — Philippians 1:9, 10.

VIII. TO BE LOVING — I Thessalonians 3:12, 13.

IX. TO BE MODERATE OR GENTLE — Philippians 4:5.

X. TO BE ABIDING — I John 2:28.

XI. TO BE AN EXAMPLE — I Peter 5:1-4.

XII. TO BE PERSEVERING — Revelation 2:25; 3:11.

XIII. TO BE SOBER, RIGHTEOUS, AND GODLY — Titus 2:11-14.

XIV. TO BE LOVING HIS APPEARING — II Timothy 4:8.

XV. TO BE A TRUE DISCIPLE — Matthew 16:24-27.

XVI. TO BE SEEKING THOSE THINGS WHICH ARE ABOVE — Colossians 3:1-4.

XVII. TO BE OBSERVING THE LORD'S SUPPER — I Corinthians 11:26.

XVIII. TO BE ASSEMBLING OURSELVES TOGETHER — Hebrews 10:25.

XIX. TO BE HOLY — I Thessalonians 5:23; II Peter 3:10-14.

XX. TO BE AVOIDING HASTY JUDGMENTS — I Corinthians 4:5.

In the light of the truth that Jesus Christ may return at any time, may we be stirred by these words by John F. Walvoord, "While you and I cannot predict events, we certainly can face the fact that the Lord could come tonight. If this is true, it makes all the more urgent the question of your personal relationship to the Lord Jesus Christ. Certainly, if the rapture is imminent, it is all the more necessary to face the fact that now is the time to receive Jesus Christ as personal Saviour. Now is the time for Christians to face the task of evangelism, prayer, devotion and service."

WHAT THE TRUTH OF THE LORD'S SECOND COMING DID TO ONE PASTOR AND CHURCH

In the early years of his Christian ministry, P. W. Philpott didn't believe in the premillennial return of Christ. He believed that the church would save the whole world, taking the world for Christ! His courage weakened, however, as he observed "evil men and seducers waxing worse and worse, deceiving, and being deceived" (II Tim. 3:13). Then a change occurred! He heard a stirring message on the second coming of Christ. The message was sane and Scriptural. Said he, "The message gripped my soul and set it on fire for the lost ones. From the study of God's Word, I saw that the mission of the church is not to take the world for Christ, *but to take Christ to the world!* Rarely in my teaching and preaching did I fail to emphasize this verse: 'And now, little children, abide in him; that when he shall appear, we may have confidence, and not be ashamed before him at his coming' (I John 2:28). The church I was serving at the time grew from 50 believers to more than 2,000. Of that number 16 young people were converted and went forth as foreign missionaries! Souls were saved in increasing numbers, and Christians were cleansed from sin. How could it have been otherwise when God's Word says: 'And every man that hath this hope in him purifieth himself, even as he is pure' (I John 3:3)?"

IT IS THE LAST HOUR

The sunset burns across the sky; upon the air, its warning cry
    The curfew tolls, from tower to tower, O children, 'tis the last, last hour!
The work that centuries might have done must crowd the hour of setting sun;
    And through all lands the saving Name ye must, in fervent haste, proclaim.
The fields are white to harvest. Weep, O tardy reapers, as ye reap,
    For wasted hours that might have won rich harvest ere the set of sun.
We hear His footsteps on the way! O work, while it is called today,
    Constrained by love, endued with power, O children, in this last, last hour!

— R. A. Brown

UNIT XLIII
"WHAT HE WANTS ME TO *BE*"

Norman J. Clayton has written a beautiful song entitled "Every Moment of Every Day," in which are found these words:

"Only to be what He wants me to be, every moment of every day."

I would like to share with you what I found in the Bible as to what He wants me to *be*. God wants everyone of us to know this, because, as Walter Wilson says, "God is more interested in making you what you ought to *be* than in giving you what you think you want."

God wants me, and you, to:

I. *BE* SAVED — John 3:17; 10:9; Acts 16:30, 31; Romans 10:9, 13.

Many times in the Bible God makes it clear to us that He wants us to be saved.

II. *BE* BAPTIZED — Acts 10:48.

In this verse God commands those who are saved to be baptized. In the Great Commission given in Matthew 28:19, 20, Jesus commands us to "Go ye therefore, and teach [disciple] all nations, baptizing them in the name of the Father, and of the Son, and of the Holy Ghost."

III. *BE* STEADFAST — I Corinthians 15:58.

In Acts 2:41, 42, it says of the early Christians after they were baptized, "And they continued steadfastly in the apostle's doctrine and fellowship, and in breaking of bread, and in prayers."

IV. *BE* SEPARATED — II Corinthians 6:17.

God wants His children separated from sin and unto Himself.

V. *BE* WITNESSING — Acts 1:8.

God has given us His Holy Spirit to empower us for a life of witnessing, starting at home, and going to the uttermost part of the earth.

VI. *BE* READY — Matthew 24:44.

We should be ready for the coming again of Jesus Christ because He may come at any moment.

VII. *BE* SPIRIT-FILLED — Ephesians 5:18.

God commands every Christian to be filled with (controlled by) the Holy Spirit.

Will you honestly say, "I want to be what He wants me to be"? Only as a person is saved and Spirit-filled will he be that kind of person. May it be true of you and me.

HIS LIFE CHANGED BY HIS OWN MESSAGE

J. Wilbur Chapman, well-known evangelist, often narrated the following incident: When he was fulfilling the work of the ministry at Wannamaker Church, Philadelphia, he became so discouraged with the lack of results that one Monday morning, he began to write a letter of resignation. He felt that he should return to a business life rather than fail to meet the requirements of that important sphere.

"While the ink was still wet," he said, "the servant brought in the morning newspaper which contained an address of my own delivered at the Northfield Conference in which I had happened to say that 'the work which really counts is not that which we do for God, but which He does through us!'"

Chapman said the reading of that sentence again revolutionized his life. As soon as the servant had retired, he knelt at his table and asked that from that hour his whole nature might be so absolutely at God's disposal as to *be* the pure channel for the living water. To do God's will became henceforward the origin, the motive, and the gladness of his life.

GOD'S BEST

God has His best things for the few who dare to stand the test;
God has His second choice for those who will not have His best.
It is not always open ill that risks the Promised Rest;
The better often is the foe that keeps us from God's Best.
Some seek the highest choice, but, when by trials pressed,
They shrink, they yield, they shun the cross and so they lose God's
     best.
Give me, O Lord, Thy highest choice, let others take the rest;
Their good things have no charm for me, I want Thy very best.
I want, in this short life of mine, as much as can be pressed
Of service true for God and man; make me to be Thy best.

— A. B. Simpson

UNIT XLIV
WHAT IF CHRIST CAME BEFORE CHRISTMAS?

Some time ago, in the Good News Broadcaster, Theodore Epp wrote an editorial entitled, "Will Jesus Come before Christmas?" in which he said, "I am aware that this title may arouse suspicion of date setting. Far be this from us! However, I am convinced that we are living so apathetically that we fail to realize that He could actually come before Christmas. . . . "

As I read this, the thought came to me — What if Christ came before Christmas? If Christ came before Christmas:

I. MANY PEOPLE WOULD BE SURPRISED.

There are many people who do not believe Jesus will return, many who are not looking for Him, many who would not be ready if He should return. Surely there will be hundreds of millions of people living on the earth who will be very surprised when He comes.

II. ALL TRUE CHRISTIANS WOULD BE TAKEN OUT OF THE WORLD.

When Jesus returns for His own, all true Christians will be taken out of the world "in the twinkling of an eye" (I Thess. 4:16, 17; I Cor. 15:51, 52).

III. ALL THE UNSAVED WOULD BE LEFT ON THE EARTH.

There will be a great separation of the saved and unsaved at His coming, all the saved being taken and all the unsaved being left on the earth (Matthew 24:37-44; Luke 17:26-36).

IV. ALL OPPORTUNITIES FOR CHRISTIAN SERVICE WOULD BE OVER.

There would be no more opportunties for Christians to pray, witness, and win others to Christ, because all the Christians would be gone. "I must work the works of him that sent me, while it is day: the night cometh, when no man can work" (John 9:4).

V. ALL OPPORTUNITIES FOR SALVATION FOR THOSE WHO LOVED NOT THE TRUTH WOULD BE OVER.

II Thessalonians 2:10-12 makes it clear that all those who believed not the truth and are not saved when Christ comes again will be sent strong delusion by God and will all be damned.

Jesus may come today — better be ready today (Matt. 24:44). Repent and receive Christ now, so that you will be ready when He comes (Acts 20:21; John 1:12).

"I WANT TO BE READY WHEN THE LORD COMES"

Recently I read a tract about the Second Coming of Jesus. It told the story of young John who was a servant-boy to a rich doctor in London. John's master loved the Lord Jesus Christ and often had church meetings in the large living room of his home. At one of these meetings the doctor talked about the coming again of the Lord Jesus to take to Heaven all those who believe in Him. Everyone else would be left behind.

After the meeting was over, the doctor said, "Well, John, I just want to tell you that if Jesus comes before I die, I shall no longer want the things I now have. He will take me away with Him and then you may have my house and all my money."

Such an offer took John by surprise. He could only stammer out his thanks. That night he lay awake wondering why his master had offered him all that wealth. Suddenly he thought, "Why should I want a house and furniture, a car, horses, and money after the Lord comes? How terrible it would be to be left behind, even if all my master's belongings were mine!"

Soon he could bear the thought no longer. He slipped out of bed, ran quickly down the hall to the room where his master slept and knocked on the door.

"Why, John," asked the doctor, "what's the matter? What do you want?" "Please sir," answered John, "I don't want your house after the Lord comes, or your car, or horses, or money."

"Well, John, what *do* you want?"

"Oh sir, I want to be ready when the Lord comes, to go with Him to Heaven." Right there in the doctor's bedroom, John put his trust in the Lord Jesus Christ and was saved and knew that he was ready for the Lord's coming.

WHAT WOULD HE SAY?

If He should come today and find my hands so full
Of future plans, however fair, in which my Saviour has no share,
        What would He say?
If He should come today and find my love so cold,
My faith so very weak and dim I had not even looked for Him,
        What would He say?
If He should come today would I be glad — quite glad?
Remembering He had died for all and none, thru me, had heard His
  call,
        What would I say?

                — Grace E. Troy

UNIT XLV
WHAT TIME IS IT?
Romans 13:11-14

Zeke Jones, the farmer, had two small boys. One winter day when they were house-bound, these two boys decided to take the mantel clock apart and put it together again. Early the next morning, Zeke was astonished to hear the clock striking 87 times without a break. He shouted in amazement, "Wake up, Maw! Get up, boys! It's later than we think, later than I ever heard it before!"

In the passage of Scripture above, God answers the question; What time is it?

I. IT IS TIME TO WAKE UP.

"And that knowing the time, that now it is high time to awake out of sleep . . ." (Rom. 13:11). Many Christians are spiritually asleep — inactive, doing nothing; ignorant, knowing nothing; and insensible, feeling nothing. God says it's time to wake up:

A. Because Christ is coming — "now is our salvation nearer than when we believed" (v. 11). The words "our salvation" refer to the future tense of salvation, when Jesus Christ comes to take His own to Himself. Yes, His coming is near "even at the doors" (Matt. 24:33).

B. Because the hour is late — "The night is far spent, the day is at hand . . . " (Rom. 13:12). Charles L. Feinberg, Dean of Talbot Theoligical Seminary, recently stated, "The world is in its last Saturday night whirl. Yes, it is later than any one of us thinks. It is not just our fundamentalist preachers telling us that; it is educators and scientists and statesmen who are saying that time is running out."

II. IT IS TIME TO CLEAN UP.

God's Word tells us "let us therefore cast off the works of darkness. . . . Let us walk honestly . . . not in rioting and drunkenness, not in chambering and wantonness, not in strife and envying" (Rom. 13:12, 13). It is time to clean up our lives.

III. IT IS TIME TO DRESS UP.

God commands us: "let us put on the armour of light. . . . But put ye on the Lord Jesus Christ . . . " (Rom. 13:12, 14).

John Calvin said, "To put on Christ means our being surrounded and protected in every part by the virtue of His Spirit, and thus rendered fit for the performance of every duty of holiness." One version renders verse 14: "Let us be Christ's men from head to foot."

"CLOSING TIME, GENTLEMEN"

E. Schuyler English, Editor-in-Chief of the Pilgrim Edition Bible, related this recently in his magazine, *The Pilgrim*:

About a century ago a group of scientists in Paris, during an after-dinner conversation, was speculating about the future. Pierre Berthelot, an eminent chemist, predicted that by the year 1969 "man would know of what the atom is constituted and would be able, at will, to moderate, extinguish, and light up the sun." The most distinguished physiologist of that era, Claude Bernard, saw a future in which "man would be so completely the master of organic law that he would create life in competition with God." The famous de Goncourt brothers were present on that occasion, and one of them remarked at a later date in their *Journal*: "To all this we raised no objection. But we have the feeling that when this time comes to science God . . . will come down to earth . . . and will say to humanity, the way they say 'Five o'clock' at the salon: 'Closing time, gentlemen!'"

STIR UNTO FLAME

Stir me! oh, stir me, Lord I care not how,
    But stir my heart in passion for the world.
Stir me to give, to go — but most to pray,
    Stir 'til the blood-red banner be unfurled
O'er lands that still in heathen darkness lie,
    Lands where the Cross was never lifted high.
Stir me! oh, stir me, Lord, Thy heart was stirred
    By love's intensest fire, 'til Thou didst give
Thine only Son, Thy best beloved One,
    E'en to the dreadful Cross, that I might live.
Stir me to give myself so back to Thee
    That Thou canst give Thyself again through me.
Stir me! oh, stir me, Lord, for I can see
    The final glorious triumph day to break!
The dawn already gilds the eastern sky,
    Oh, Church of Christ, arise! awake, awake!
Oh, stir us Lord, as heralds of that day,
    For night is past — our King is on His way!
                — Bessie Porter Head

UNIT XLVI
WHAT TO DO WITH YOURSELF

A well-known writer made this statement "The great enemy of the modern world, 'Public Enemy No. 1', is boredom. . . . I repeat: despite all appearances, mankind is bored. Perhaps this is the underlying cause of all our troubles. We no longer know what to do with ourselves." Let me give you three things God tells us to do with ourselves.

I. SEARCH YOURSELF.

God says in II Corinthians 13:5: "Examine *yourselves* . . . prove your *own selves*. Know ye not your *own selves,* how that Jesus Christ is in you, except ye be reprobates?" "Examine . . . prove . . . know." In these three words, God is saying to you, "Search yourself," to see if you are really saved, because you may find that you are only a counterfeit. The Amplified New Testament translates the last few words of II Corinthians 13:5: "Unless you are counterfeits." I have met many counterfeits in my ministry. Look up these verses in I John and search yourself to see whether you have really been born again: I John 2:3-5; 2:29; 3:9; 3:24; 4:7; 5:1; 5:4, 5. If you find that you have never truly been saved, then God says:

II. SAVE YOURSELF.

God's Word instructs us in Acts 2:40: "Save *yourselves* from this untoward generation." Of course, no one can really save himself, but he can come to God in "repentance toward God, and faith toward our Lord Jesus Christ" (Acts 20:21), and God will save him. He promises, "Believe on the Lord Jesus Christ, and thou shalt be saved, and thy house" (Acts 16:31). The Amplified New Testament puts it like this: "Be saved from this crooked [perverse] generation." After you are saved, then God tells you:

III. SURRENDER YOURSELF.

In Romans 6:13 God beseeches us: "yield *yourselves* unto God. . . ." Yield means to surrender.

William Borden surrendered himself to God and wrote these words in his prayer of consecration: "Lord Jesus, I take hands off, as far as my life is concerned. I put Thee on the throne in my heart. Change, cleanse, use me as Thou shalt choose. I take the full power of Thy Holy Spirit. I thank Thee." His biographer wrote of Him: "No reserve, no retreat, no regrets had any place in Borden's consecration to God."

THE END OF JOHN WESLEY'S SEARCH

John Wesley was the son of pious parents; his father was a minister and his mother was one of the most amazing mothers who ever lived, a very godly woman. As a young man he lived a holy life, partook of the Lord's Supper weekly, gave alms to the poor, prayed, fasted, joined the Holy Club at Oxford University, became a minister and came to Savannah, Georgia to preach to the Indians. After two years as a missionary in America, he set sail for England. "What have I learned?" he asked himself when he once again was on English soil. "Why, I have learned what I least of all suspected, that I, who went to America to convert the Indians, was never myself converted to God!" After searching for peace for many years, at the age of thirty-five, on May 24, 1738, his search came to an end. He recorded in his famous journal: "In the evening I went very unwillingly to the society in Aldersgate Street, where one was reading Luther's Preface to the Epistle to the Romans. About a quarter before nine, while he was describing the change which God works in the heart through faith in Christ, I felt my heart strangely warmed. I felt I did trust in Christ, Christ alone, for salvation; and an assurance was given me that He had taken away *my* sins, even *mine,* and saved *me* from the law of sin and death."

CROWNED OR CRUCIFIED

I stood alone at the bar of God, in the hush of the twilight dim,
　And faced the question that pierced my heart: "What will you do with Him?
Crowned or crucified? Which shall it be?" No other choice was offered me.
　He held out His loving hands to me, while He pleadingly said, "Obey;
Make Me thy choice, for I love thee so," and I could not say to Him, nay.
　Crowned, not crucified, this it must be; no other way was open to me.
I knelt in tears at the feet of Christ, in the hush of the twilight dim,
　And all that I was, or hoped, or sought, surrendered unto Him.
Crowned, not crucified — my heart shall know no King but Christ, who loveth me so.

— Anonymous

UNIT XLVII
WHAT YOU NEED IS WHAT CHRIST OFFERS
Philippians 4:19

Just as every person has certain physical needs to keep him physically well, so every person has certain spiritual needs to keep him spiritually well. The Word of God promises in Philippians 4:19: "But my God shall supply all your need according to his riches in glory by Christ Jesus." Here are some of our spiritual needs and how God and Christ will meet them.

We need:

I. CLEANSING.

God says, "But we are all as an unclean thing . . ." (Isa. 64:6). In order for us to have our sins cleansed, we must repent of our sins and put our trust in the Lord Jesus Christ who died for our sins. Then we can claim His promise: "and the blood of Jesus Christ his Son cleanseth us from all sin" (I John 1:7).

II. HAPPINESS.

Every person longs for happiness and joy. Christ offers us His joy: "These things have I spoken unto you, that my joy might remain in you, and that your joy might be full" (John 15:11).

III. REST.

The great quest of people today is rest or peace of heart and mind. Christ offers to meet this need of our life. Listen to His sweet invitation: "Come unto me, all ye that labor and are heavy laden, and I will give you *rest*" (Matt. 11:28).

IV. INSTRUCTION.

Here is a wonderful and blessed offer of instruction: 'I will *instruct thee* and teach thee in the way which thou shalt go: I will guide thee with mine eye" (Ps. 32:8).

V. SATISFACTION.

This is His offer of satisfaction: "For he satisfieth the longing soul, and filleth the hungry soul with goodness" (Ps. 107:9).

VI. TRIUMPH.

Christ's offer of victory is found in II Corinthians 2:14: "Now thanks be unto God, which always causes us to *triumph* in Christ. . . ."

When we have Christ as our personal Saviour and Lord we can say with the song writer, "All Things in Jesus I Find."

JESUS IS ENOUGH

H. A. Ironside relates this interesting story:

In a hospital ward a lady missionary found an undersized and undeveloped little Irish boy, whose white, wizened face and emaciated form excited her deepest sympathy. Perhaps he was of about fifteen years of age; he scarcely looked to be twelve. Winning the lad's confidence by gifts and flowers and fruit, she soon found him very willing, and even eager, to listen to the story of the sinner's Saviour. At first his interest seemed of an impersonal character, but gradually he began to be immediately concerned. His own soul's need was put before him, and he was awakened to some sense of his lost condition, insomuch that he commenced seriously to consider how he might be saved. Brought up a Romanist, he thought and spoke of penance and confessional, of sacraments and church, yet never wholly leaving out Christ Jesus and His atoning work.

One morning the lady called again upon him, and found his face aglow with a new-found joy. Inquiring the reason, he replied with assurance born of faith in the revealed Word of God, "O missis, I always knew that Jesus was necessary; but I never knew till yesterday that He was enough!"

It was a blessed discovery, and I would that every reader of these pages had made it. Mark it well: Jesus is enough!

"Who of God is made unto us wisdom, and righteousness, and sanctification, and redemption." "Ye are complete in him." "God hath made us accepted in the beloved." These are only a few of the precious declarations of Scripture which show clearly that Jesus is indeed not only necessary, but enough.

JESUS IS ALL I NEED

When I am burdened, or weary and sad, Jesus is all I need;
   Never He fails to uplift and make glad, Jesus is all I need.
When I am swept by the tempests of life, Jesus is all I need;
   Peace He imparts, whatsoever the strife, Jesus is all I need.
When thro' the valley He calls me to go, Jesus is all I'll need;
   He will be with me to cheer me, I know, Jesus is all I'll need.
All that I need He will always be, all that I need till His face I see;
   All that I need thro' eternity, Jesus is all I need.

— James Rowe

UNIT XLVIII
WHAT YOU'RE GOING TO GET
Luke 18:14

One night Harry Ironside was standing in the rear of the auditorium of the Meeting Hall when he heard two men talking. One said, "Have you noticed the difference between the preaching of Loizeaux and Ironside?"

The other man replied, "There is no way to compare the two; they are so utterly different."

The first man said, "Yes, but there is one thing that stands out prominently. When Paul Loizeaux preaches, he's always telling people what they're going to get when they come to Christ. But Harry Ironside is always telling them what they're going to get if they don't."

In this message, I desire to be like both of these men. Like Loizeaux, I want to tell you what you'll get when you come to Christ. Like Ironside, I want to tell you what you'll get if you don't come to Christ.

I. IF YOU COME TO CHRIST, YOU'LL GET REST.

Jesus promises, "Come unto me, all ye that labor and are heavy laden, and I will give you rest" (Matt. 11:28-30). He offers us "peace with God" (Rom. 5:1), and "the peace of God" (Phil. 4:6, 7).

II. IF YOU DON'T COME TO CHRIST, YOU'LL GET REST-LESSNESS.

God's Word says, "But the wicked are like the troubled sea, when it cannot rest.... There is no peace, saith my God, to the wicked" (Isa. 57:20, 21).

III. IF YOU COME TO CHRIST, YOU'LL GET LIFE.

A. Eternal life (John 3:16, 36; 5:24; 10:27-29; Rom. 6:23; I John 5:11-13).

B. Abundant life (John 10:10).

IV. IF YOU DON'T COME TO CHRIST, YOU'LL GET DEATH.

A. Physical (Rom. 5:12; Heb. 9:27).

B. Spiritual (Eph. 2:1; I Tim. 5:6).

C. Eternal (Rev. 20:14; 21:8).

V. IF YOU COME TO CHRIST, YOU'LL GET HEAVEN — John 14:1-6; Revelation 21:1-7; 22:1-5.

VI. IF YOU DON'T COME TO CHRIST, YOU'LL GET HELL — Psalm 9:17; Matthew 10:28; 25:41, 46; Mark 9:43-48; Luke 16:19-31; Revelation 20:14; 21:8.

In the text, Luke 18:41, Jesus asked, "What wilt thou that I shall do unto thee?" Come to Christ, receive Him as your Saviour and Lord, and you will get rest, life, and heaven.

HE GOT HELL BECAUSE HE JUST PUT IT OFF

Dr. Martin, a pastor in Texas, had a friend, George, who was a rich, unsaved lawyer. He had an accident and was dying in a hospital. Dr. Martin visited him, pleaded with him to become a Christian. George raised his hand and whispered, "Ah, Martin, I am sorry, but it's too late, it's too late. Martin, if somebody had come to me ten years ago, ten months ago, ten hours ago, to say, 'George, you are going to die and go to hell,' I would have said, 'Man, you are crazy. I'm not an infidel. I believe in Christ. I expect to accept Him as my personal Saviour.' Yet, here I am, dying a lost sinner, going to hell, because I just put it off, I guess."

Dr. Martin said, tears pouring down his cheeks, "The best friend I had in the world lived a Christless life. He died a Christless death. We put him in a Christless coffin. We had a Christless funeral. We buried him in a Christless grave. He will face a Christless judgment. He will sink into a Christless hell, because he put it off."

WHAT THEN?

TO THE UNBELIEVER

After the joys of earth,
After its songs of mirth,
After its hours of light,
After its dreams so bright —
   What then?

Only an empty name,
Only a weary frame,
Only a conscious smart,
Only an aching heart —
   What then?

Only a sad farewell
To a world loved too well,
Only a silent bed
With the forgotten dead —
   What then?

After this sad farewell
To a world loved too well,
After this silent bed
With the forgotten dead —
   What then?

Oh! then — the judgment-throne!
Oh! then — the last hope — gone!
Then, all the woes that dwell
In an eternal Hell!

TO THE BELIEVER

After the Christian's tears,
After his fights and fears,
After his weary cross,
"All things below but loss" —
   What then?

Oh! then — a holy calm,
Resting on Jesus' arm,
Oh! then — a deeper love
For the pure home above —
   What then?

Oh! then — work for Him,
Perishing souls to win,
Then Jesus' presence near,
Death's darkest hour to cheer —
   What then?

And when the work is done,
When the last soul is won,
When Jesus' love and power
Brings the expected hour —
   What then?

Oh! then — the crown is given!
Oh! then — the rest in Heaven!
Endless life, in endless day,
Sin and sorrow passed away.

UNIT XLIX
WHO'S WHO IN HELL

There are many names in *Who's Who, Who's Who in America, Who's Who in U.S.S.R., Who's Who in the Bible,* plus over thirty other books titled *Who's Who,* but in this message I want you to see those who are going to hell, "Who's Who in Hell."

I. THE PEOPLE WHO ARE NOT SAVED WHEN JESUS RETURNS TO EARTH — Matthew 25:31-46.

When Jesus returns to earth at the close of the Great Tribulation, He will say to those who are unsaved who are living on the earth at that time, "Depart from me, ye cursed, into everlasting fire, prepared for the devils and his angels" (Matt. 25:41).

II. THE BEAST AND FALSE PROPHET — Revelation 19:20.

These are two men who will be empowered by Satan during the Great Tribulation. They will both be cast alive into the lake of fire and "shall be tormented day and night forever and ever" (Rev. 20:10).

III. THE PEOPLE WHO WORSHIP THE BEAST AND HIS IMAGE — Revelation 14:9-11.

It is said of these people, they "shall be tormented with fire and brimstone . . . " (Rev. 14:9-11).

IV. THE DEVIL — Revelation 20:10; Matthew 25:41.

The devil will be cast into the lake of fire and shall be tormented day and night forever and ever.

V. THE FALLEN ANGELS — II Peter 2:4; Matthew 25:41.

These are the angels who followed Satan, the devil, in his rebellion against God. (See also Jude 6.)

VI. THE FEARFUL, UNBELIEVING, ABOMINABLE, MURDERERS, WHOREMONGERS, SORCERERS, IDOLATORS AND ALL LIARS — Revelation 21:8.

Eight different classes of people are mentioned in this list who will have their part in the lake of fire and brimstone.

VII. THE PEOPLE WHOSE NAMES ARE NOT WRITTEN IN THE BOOK OF LIFE — Revelation 20:15.

God's Word says that some names are written in the book of life (Luke 10:20; Phil. 4:3), others are not (Rev. 13:8; 17:8; 20:15).

If you are not saved, you should immediately repent of your sins (Luke 13:3), and believe on the Lord Jesus Christ (John 3:16), so that you will not perish, or go to hell. I pray you will do it right now before it is too late.

FORTY-EIGHT HOURS IN HELL

John W. Reynolds tells the story of a miner, George Lennox, who was a notorious character, and was serving his second term in prison. On day as he was working in the mine he was completely covered when the roof fell on him. He was pronounced dead by a physician, and as he was being prepared for burial, his body was dropped. To the amazement of all present, he groaned, his eyes opened, and other appearances of life were manifested. He was taken to the hospital where he stayed six months, and later went back to work.

Mr. Reynolds asked him about the time during which he was unconscious, and Lennox told him: "It seemed as if a great iron door swung open, and I passed through it. The thought came to my mind that I was dead and in another world. I was taken by a being utterly impossible to describe to a place where I saw on the wall these words 'This is hell.' I traveled through darkness, and heard groans and the cry for 'Water, water, water.' I beheld the lake of fire where hugh billows of fire would roll over each other and saw human beings carried down to the lowest depths of this awful lake of fire.

"I passed through all this, and I am well satisfied that there is an old-fashioned hell. But there is one thing certain; I am never going to that place any more. As soon as I opened my eyes in the hospital, and found that I was alive and on earth once more, I immediately trusted Jesus Christ as my personal Saviour, and I am going to live and die a Christian."

A VOICE FROM HELL

You lived next door to me for years, we shared our dreams, our joys and tears.
  A friend to me you were indeed, a friend who helped me when in need.
What sadness, then my friend, to find, that after all, you weren't so kind.
  The day my life on earth did end I found you weren't a faithful friend.
For all those years we spent on earth, you never talked of second birth.
  You never spoke of my lost soul and of the Christ who'd make me whole!
But do not err, my friend, again — do all you can for souls of men.
  Plead with them now quite earnestly, lest they be cast in hell with me!

UNIT L
THE "WHY GENERATION"

Teen-agers have been called the "Lost Generation" by Gertrude Stein; the "Open Generation" by *Look* magazine; the "Tormented Generation" by *Holiday* magazine; the "Beat Generation"; the "Now Generation"; the "In Generation"; the "Twisted Generation"; the "Uncommitted Generation"; and the "Why Generation."

Too many of them are like the college freshman who wrote: "*Why* have I struggled and wasted my years and tears, and thought, and actions? We are ready to die at birth. Where do we go from here? Some even seek something later. What fools! *Why* am I here for this short span of years? Life is useless. I torture myself to find meaning. Oh! How sick I am."

God's Word tells us why He has put us here. Let me give the "Why Generation" three reasons the Bible reveals as to *why you are here.*

I. YOU ARE HERE TO BRING PLEASURE TO GOD.

Revelation 4:11 speaks of people casting their crowns before the throne and saying: "Thou are worthy, O Lord, to receive glory and honor and power: for thou hast created all things, and *for thy pleasure they are and were created.*" We are here to bring pleasure to God. We can only do that:

A. By being saved (Rom. 8:8; Heb. 11:6; Acts 16:31).

B. By being surrendered (Rom. 12:1, 2).

Only as a person is saved by believing on the Lord Jesus Christ as personal Saviour and Lord, and surrendering himself to God as a living sacrifice, can he please God. ("acceptable unto God" in Romans 12:1 is rendered "well-pleasing to God" in the A.N.T.).

II. YOU ARE HERE TO BRING PRAISE TO GOD.

In Psalm 102:18, God says, "*. . . the people which shall be created shall praise the Lord.*" Look up and read Psalm 50:23a; 69:30, 31; 107:8, 15, 21, 31; 146-150; Hebrews 13:15, 16.

III. YOU ARE HERE TO BRING GLORY TO GOD.

God says, "*I have created him for my glory. . . .* (Isa. 43:71, and in I Corinthians 10:31: "Whether therefore ye eat, or drink, or whatsoever ye do, *do all to the glory of God.*"

May your life bring pleasure, praise, and glory to God.

PETE AND BOB FOUND PURPOSE IN LIVING

Jack Wyrtzen tells about two brothers who found purpose in living:

Back in the spring of 1950, one Sunday afternoon, into our West Point Bible class came a stranger, a young fellow that had never attended our class before. I noticed the fellows nudging one another and under their breath saying, "Pete Monfore, Pete Monfore." I said, "Excuse me, who is Pete Monfore around here?" "If you'd follow boxing a little more carefully you'd know who he is. He's the eastern intercollegiate boxing champ."

Some of the fellows persuaded him to come to Bible class the next week and the next week and the next. One day we were having a testimony meeting and old Pete got to his feet and said, "Most of you fellows know me as a fighter, but I want you to know that the other day I gave my heart to Jesus Christ, and from here on out I'm going to be fighting the good fight of faith."

Then came the word *Korea* and within a month Pete Monfore was company commander on the front lines of Korea. It wasn't too many weeks before the war ended that Pete Monfore had been leading his own company up on top of Heartbreak Ridge, fighting the Communists, and the enemy artillery opened up. When the smoke and dust had settled, they found the remains of Pete Monfore's body. The Medics went through his uniform and in his pocket they found a little bloodstained New Testament. They opened it and read on the fly leaf: "Pete Monfore, Philippians 1:21." Then he had scribbled a note, "If anything happens to me, I would like this New Testament sent to my brother Bob at Northwestern University." From Korea to Northwestern University came this blood stained New Testament.

Bob was a skeptic, who mocked and laughed at the things of God. When he read "Pete Monfore, Philippians 1:21" he wondered what Philippians 1:21 meant. As he looked through his brother's Testament he found the verse underlined: "For to me to live is Christ, and to die is gain." Before Bob Monfore had finished reading through the New Testament, he got on his knees and prayed, "O God, I'm a sinner, but I believe Jesus died and rose again. Lord, come into my heart." If you should ask Bob Monfore, who is a ranch owner out west today, what his testimony is, he would say, "The same as my brother Peter, 'For to me to live is Christ, and to die is gain'."

WORK OUT THY PURPOSE IN MY LIFE

Work out Thy purpose in my life, whate'er that purpose be;
Dear Lord, I give myself to Thee; may grace produce in me
The Christ life, and His image dear a dying world need see.
— Bernice Goertz

UNIT LI
WHY THERE ARE NOT MORE SOUL-WINNERS

As the Personal Evangelism instructor at a Bible Institute for seven and one-half years, I read many books on this subject. I read a number of times in these books that 95 per cent of Christians never win a soul to Christ.

There are three main reasons why there are not more soul-winners:

I. THERE IS A LACK OF CONVICTION THAT PEOPLE ARE LOST.

A recent survey by George Gallup discovered that 46 per cent of the American people do not believe in hell.

People who die without Christ as their personal Saviour are lost and will be in hell for all eternity, according to God's Word. His Word speaks of those who are lost (II Cor. 4:3, 4); who are condemned already (John 3:18); who have the wrath of God abiding on them (John 3:36); "Who shall be punished with everlasting destruction from the presence of the Lord, and from the glory of his power" (II Thess. 1:9).

II. THERE IS A LACK OF CONCERN FOR THE LOST.

Bishop Taylor lamented, "It seems we have lost a word out of our Christian vocabulary — the word *concern*." Many people all about us could echo the cry of the psalmist when he cried out, "no man cared for my soul" (Ps. 142:4).

A. Jeremiah had concern (Jer. 9:1).
B. Paul had concern (Rom. 9:1-3).
C. Jesus had concern (Matt. 9:36).
D. May God give us concern (Ps. 126:6).

III. THERE IS A LACK OF CONSECRATION OF LIFE.

Mr. Johnson has said, "The chief obstacle to the spread of Christianity is not Hinduism, Buddhism, nor even paganism, but the rotten behaviour of people who call themselves Christians." God has said, "be ye clean, that bear the vessels of the Lord" (Isa. 52:11).

In Romans 12:1 God says, "I beseech you therefore brethren, by the mercies of God, that ye present your bodies a living sacrifice, holy, acceptable unto God, which is your reasonable service." It is only as our lives are consecrated, dedicated to God, that He can use us as He wishes to win souls.

May God help us to be convicted of the lostness of people, concerned about them, and consecrated to God to win them to Christ before it is too late.

AN INFIDEL'S TESTIMONY WHICH CHANGED C. T. STUDD

An Infidel's Testimony: Did I firmly believe, as millions say they do, that the knowledge and practice of religion in this life influences destiny in another, religion would be to me everything. I would cast aside earthly enjoyments as dross, earthly cares as follies, and earthly thoughts and feelings as vanity. Religion would be my first waking thought and my last image before sleep sank me into unconsciousness. I would labor in its cause alone. I would take thought for the morrow of eternity alone. I would esteem one soul gained for heaven worth a life of suffering. Earthly consequence would never stay my hand nor seal my lips. Earth, its joy and its griefs, would occupy no moment of my thoughts. I would strive to look upon eternity alone, and on the immortal souls around me, soon to be everlastingly miserable or everlastingly happy. I would go forth to the world and preach to it in season and out of season, and my text would be Mark 8:36, "What shall it profit a man if he shall gain the whole world and lose his own soul?"

A Christian's Testimony: When C. T. Studd, the great Cambridge cricketer of England, read the infidel's words, they made such a tremendous impression upon him that he gave up a legal career to go to the dark places of the earth as a missionary. Studd says, "The infidel's words decided me at once to live only and utterly for Christ."

While studying the Bible one day, Mr. Studd applied the story of the rich young ruler to himself and gave away his entire fortune, a half million dollars, and followed Christ in voluntary poverty to China, then India, and then at the age of 50, to Africa. Studd's last term of service was in the heart of Africa for nearly thirteen years without a furlough. In great affliction of body, Studd translated the New Testament and part of the Old into Kingwana, and then passed on to be with his Lord.

OPEN MY EYES

Open my eyes, that I may see, this one and that one needing Thee:
  Hearts that are dumb, unsatisfied; lives that are dark, for whom
    Christ died.
Open my eyes in sympathy clear into man's deep soul to see;
  Wise with Thy wisdom to discern, and with Thy heart of love to
    yearn.
Open my eyes in power, I pray give me the strength to speak today,
  Some one to bring, dear Lord, to Thee; use me, O Lord, use even
    me.
                                    — Betty Scott Stam

UNIT LII
YOUR THREE APPOINTMENTS WITH GOD

There are many appointments we make in life, many of which we keep, some which we break. You have three appointments with God, two which you *must keep,* one which you *may keep.*

I. YOU HAVE AN APPOINTMENT WITH GOD IN DEATH.

A. It must be kept — "And as it is *appointed* unto men *once to die* . . . " (Heb. 9:27; II Sam. 14:14; Isa. 38:1; Rom. 5:12).

B. It may be this year — *"this year thou shalt die* . . . " (Jer. 28:16).

C. It may be tonight — "Thou fool, *this night thy soul shall be required of thee* . . . " (Luke 12:20).

D. It may be the next moment — *"In a moment shall they die* . . . " (Job 34:20).

E. It may be the next step — "there is but a *step between me and death"* (I Sam. 20:3).

F. It should be prepared for — *"prepare to meet thy God* . . . " (Amos 4:12).

II. YOU HAVE AN APPOINTMENT WITH GOD IN JUDGMENT.

A. All must keep it — "And as *it is appointed* unto men once to die, but *after this the judgment"* (Heb. 9:27; Acts 17:30; Rom. 14:12).

B. All must be faced — "For God shall bring *every work into judgment,* with every secret thing; whether it be good, or whether it be evil" (Eccles. 12:14).

1. Christians at the Judgment Seat of Christ (II Cor. 5:10).

2. Unsaved at the Great White Throne Judgment (Rev. 20:11-15).

C. All should be prepared — *"prepare to meet thy God* . . . " (Amos 4:12).

III. YOU MAY HAVE AN APPOINTMENT WITH GOD IN LIFE.

A. To obtain salvation — "For God hath not *appointed us* to wrath, but *to obtain salvation* . . . " (I Thess. 5:9).

B. By Jesus Christ — "to obtain salvation *by our Lord Jesus Christ"* (I Thess. 5:9).

C. It should be kept now — "behold, *now is the accepted time;* behold, *now is the day of salvation"* (II Cor. 6:2).

If we meet God in life, repent and receive Jesus Christ as our personal Saviour and Lord (Luke 13:3; Acts 16:31), then we shall obtain salvation, and we can face the other two appointments with God without fear.

A TEEN-AGER KEEPS AN APPOINTMENT WITH GOD

Recently I read this true story of a teen-ager who met God in life and obtained "salvation by our Lord Jesus Christ" (I Thess. 5:9):

"Mother, please," exploded the Scottish teen-ager. "I've heard all the religion business I can take. You and Daddy are always bothering me about it. I'm not interested!" The girl stamped her foot and marched out of the room, slamming the door.

Her mother sank wearily to a chair. What more could she do? Finally she decided to call the pastor. Thomas Chalmers received her cordially, and listened while she sobbed out her problem. Then he said, "May I talk to the lassie alone?"

An appointment was made for the pastor to call at the home. The parents left the room and Chalmers turned to the girl sympathetically. "I think it's a shame," he said, "that your mother and father pester you so about religion." The girl, who had been braced for a lecture, smiled in relief. Now this is the kind of preacher I could like, she thought. He's willing to let me alone if I'm not interested.

"I have a suggestion that may help," the pastor went on. "Suppose I consult with your parents and friends and persuade them not to mention the subject of salvation to you for a whole year." The girl was startled. "A year," she gasped. "I don't know whether it would be safe to wait a whole year. I might die before then." "That's true," agreed Chalmers. "A year's too long. Suppose we make it six months?"

The girl pondered a moment and then replied that six months might not be safe either. "Well, then," proposed the pastor, "how about three months? I'll arrange it so you won't be bothered about salvation for three months."

Chalmers arose and started to leave but the girl detained him. "I don't think it would be safe," she said, "to put it off for three months. I don't think it would be safe to put it off at all. Please pray for me now." Promptly Dr. Chalmers led her to the Saviour.

OUT OF THIS LIFE

Out of this life I shall never take things of silver and gold I make.

All that I cherish and hoard away, after I leave, on earth must stay.

And I wonder, often, just what I shall own, in that other life when I pass alone.

What shall He find and what shall He see, in the soul that answers the call for me?

Shall the great Judge learn, when my task is through that my soul had gathered some riches, too?

Or shall at the last, it be mine to find, that all I had worked for I had left behind?

OUTLINE INDEX

ILLUSTRATION INDEX

POETRY INDEX